PARIS
3 Days
No Stress

A Travel Guide

MIKE LONG

Copyright © 2017 Mike Long

All rights reserved.

ISBN: 9781520808895

DEDICATION

To Liz, Sophie, Dominic & Timo

You are my greatest gifts and
you bring immense joy to my life.

#Paris3DaysNoStress

@ParisNoStress

www.AIMLong.ca/Paris

CONTENTS

Why I Wrote This Book

Great Expectations

1	Arriving	3
2	Restaurants	15
3	Accommodations	23
4	Be Parisian	29
5	Getting Around	41
6	What to do	53
7	Starbucks	75
8	Unique Add-Ons	85
9	Misc. Tips	93
10	Taste of Things to Come	103
	About the Author	113

WHY I WROTE THIS BOOK

Not everyone can spend an entire week or longer in Paris. Perhaps you're doing an extended European trip or travelling on business and you wish to include a 2-3 day Paris-stay in your plans. Do it! Paris is always worth the little bit of extra planning and this book will make that planning even easier!

If you're like me, the traditional Paris guides can be intimidating: They're thick, heavy, and have way more detail than is necessary for a quick stay. They overwhelm me.

This book provides a manageable alternative.

I fell in love with Paris years ago, discovering it, like you, as a tourist. Since then, I've learned to make my way around with ease.

This book sums up some of the tips & tricks I've learned in the years since my first visit, in 1989, and makes them available to you to help you enjoy your time in Paris with as little stress as possible.

Not just stone-and-mortar monuments, history at every angle, or generic souvenirs, Paris is also a feeling. My goal in writing this book is to help you more easily manage the practical details so that you can focus more on experiencing the feeling; for that, dear reader, is the best souvenir you can bring home.

Happy Reading!

GREAT EXPECTATIONS

It's important that you be satisfied with your purchase and experience of this book. To ensure that, here's what you **can**, and what you **shouldn't**, expect to see in this guide.

YOU CAN EXPECT TO SEE
an overview of:

- How to get from the Airport into the city
- General information on restaurants & dining
- An introduction to accommodation options
- How to get in touch with your inner Parisian
- Options for getting around the city
- Essential monuments and attractions
- Starbucks locations near those monuments
- Unique add-ons according to your budget

HERE'S WHAT YOU WON'T SEE

- An exhaustive list of sights, restaurants or individual hotels. There are far too many to catalogue in a short volume and certainly more than you'd be able to visit in 3 days.
- Exhaustive details for individual attractions (hours of operation, pricing, etc.). These vary according to season, age, group size, etc. but I give you enough to decide whether or not you might want to include these sights in your visit.

For this reason, whenever you might need more details on a specific spot, and where possible, I'll point you to the English section of a relevant website.

MIKE LONG

1

ARRIVING

I begin by making the assumption that you are either arriving by plane or train and I divide the chapter into four sections accordingly:

1. In **Section one** I touch base on the three Greater Paris airports but focus, in detail, on Charles-de-Gaulle [CDG] as it's the biggest and most commonly used by guests arriving internationally).
2. In **section two** I'll detail your options for getting from the airport and into Paris.
3. In **section three** I'll run through the three train stations most likely to welcome international visitors and talk about transitioning to Paris' metro.
4. In **section four** I'll touch base on options for luggage storage in the city.

SECTION 1: ARRIVING BY PLANE

Depending on your flight arrangements, you may arrive at one of three airports:

1. **Charles-de-Gaulle:** (airport code **CDG**)
    - France's largest international airport
    - Principal hub for Air France
    - European hub for Delta
    - One of several European hubs for Star Alliance airlines

2. **Orly** (airport code **ORY**)
    - Secondary hub for Air France

3. **Beauvais-Tillé** (airport code **BVA**)
    - Low-cost carrier hub (for example, Ryanair, Wizz Air, etc.)

Note that in this book I'll only detail **CDG**. I transitioned through, arrived at or departed from this airport numerous times as opposed to ORY and BVA which I've never used.

CDG: OVERALL LAYOUT

There are three terminals at CDG: Terminal 1, Terminal 2 (2A-2F) and Terminal 3, however Terminal 2 makes up, by far, the largest part of the airport. I've included a diagram below, showing you the overall airport layout, including the route for CDGVAL (more on this later).

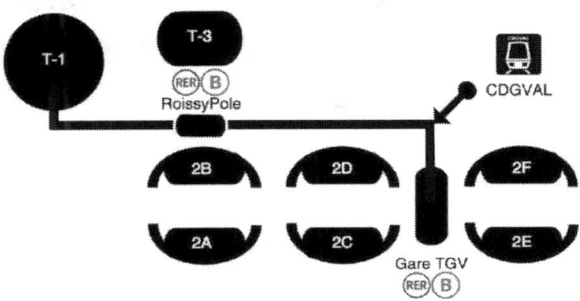

CDG: WHICH TERMINAL DO I USE?

The best way to ensure you know which terminal to use is, of course, to check your travel itinerary, ticket of boarding pass. If, however, the terminal is not indicated there, you also have the possibility of checking online, via the airport website:

EasyCDG.com/Airport-Guide
("Which Terminal")

The "Which Terminal" section of the Airport Guide will allow you to see which carriers use which terminals.

It is not a bad idea to consult this section of their site, especially if it's your first time travelling through CDG, particularly since, for some airlines, arrivals and departures do not happen at the same terminal.

As an example, both **Etihad** and **British Airways'** flights *arrive* at Terminal 2A while their check-in and departures take place in Terminal 2C.

SECTION 2:
AIRPORT TRANSFER
to and from CDG

There's another airport website that has an excellent one-page comparison of costs associated with the various means of transfer between CDG and Paris, whether by rail or by bus/coach. First, though, let me give you some of the details as well as a few of my thoughts.

www.parisaeroport.fr/en
(search for "public transport")

TRANSFER BY RAIL

Below are your options for leaving CDG by rail:

Option 1: TGV (trains à grande vitesse)

These are the high-speed, mainline trains operated by SNCF (the national rail company). The station is located between terminals 2C/2D and 2E/2F and therefore within close proximity to departures and arrivals in Terminal 2.

This option is really only of interest if, rather than going into Paris directly, you plan to bypass the capital and travel directly to another part of France.

If you *do* need to use the TGV, let me give you a bit of insight:

1. If you've not pre-purchased tickets ahead of time, you may encounter fairly long lines, depending on what time your flight arrives. It can be a very busy spot.

2. If you *have* pre-purchased tickets online (e-tickets), you should *still* allow yourself plenty of time between your arrival by air and your departure by rail. By doing so, you increase the chance of having a stress-free passage through immigration, baggage claim and international customs (the latter are usually practically non-existent). **My recommendation** is to allow yourself a minimum of one hour and thirty minutes, although even two hours is not unreasonable.

   One of the reasons I recommend a long interval time is this: rarely, if ever, have I departed OR landed on time in Paris (or at any other European airport for that matter). Air traffic is so heavy, throughout Europe, that delays in landing and takeoff are fairly routine and a 30min delay in landing can easily add a lot of stress to a tight transfer time.

3. If you *do* have pre-printed tickets, be sure to validate them in the yellow validation machines near the platform entrance.

   - By pre-printed tickets, I mean tickets printed BY the rail company. E-tickets printer on a home laser printer must bear a bar code and your name. SNCF staff will be able to assist you with any questions.

   - The yellow validation machines are called "composteurs" and you are said to "composter" (pronounced: com-pos-tay) your ticket (nothing to do with the English "compost")

Option 2: RER B

These are commuter trains operated by RATP, Paris' Transport Authority, which make up part of the overall metro/public transportation network. You can pick up the RER tickets and trains in Terminal 3 – Roissypole, located roughly 5min from Terminal 2 by CDGVAL *(below)*. When you arrive at Terminal 3 – Roissypole, simply take the escalator up to ground level where you can purchase your ticket.

The RER, in my opinion, is the service of choice for transiting from the airport to downtown. It is one of the least expensive options and takes you right into Paris' Gare du Nord (North Train Station).

Get-the-feeling tip:

If you choose to take the RER into Paris, it will be your first foray into experiencing something that many French do every day… travel by rail into the city. So throw on your shades and be nonchalant. The view, during the ride into town, will be much less glamorous than what you might expect, but it's part of the whole package.

Option 3: CDGVAL

I Only mention CDGVAL as an option here because the website offers it as a third option. However, while CDGVAL is a free, automated train shuttle, note that it **only** runs between CDG airport terminals and not into Paris.

For a map of CDGVAL, refer to the airport map above.

TRANSFER BY BUS

www.ParisAeroport.fr's website offers several city bus services that could take you into Paris as well as other coach services. With the other options available to you, ignore any city buses, there's no point given the other options available to you. As for coaches, the only one that I'm familiar with is **Roissybus**, which runs between all CDG terminals and the Opéra Garnier (metro: Opera) right downtown in the 9th arrondissement. From there you can easily move about using the metro system (which I'll get into in chapter 5).

Roissybus isn't a bad option if you are staying downtown. It's comparably priced to the RER B and puts you in the heart of the city, rather than going via the Gare du Nord. Also, Roissybus stops at all CDG terminals, meaning you don't have to worry about getting to Terminal 3 via CDGVAL first.

In my mind, it's a "six of one, a half-dozen of the other" type of scenario, but since I'm a creature of habit, I've only ever personally used the RER.

I *do* think that Roissybus could be your option of choice in the case where there were: Rail strikes with the RER personnel (which occur more frequently in France than is typical in North America), or delays on the RER line (also not entirely uncommon). Of course, you may or may not be aware of such interruptions until you have arrived, at which time know that Roissybus is an alternative.

For more information on Roissybus:
www.parisaeroport.fr and search for "Roissybus"

TRANSFER BY TAXI

While it's possible to access CDG by taxi, unless you have absolutely no other alternative, don't do it. The airport website, www.parisaeroport.fr does provide information on taxis, but given the other public transportation options, why would you? A taxi will cost a disproportionate amount of money and is more susceptible to traffic disruptions whether caused by the normal heavy traffic in the area or by protest groups who sometimes intentionally slow traffic near the airport as a means of garnering attention.

SECTION 3: ARRIVING BY RAIL

For those of you not arriving by plane, but by rail, particularly if you are traveling to Paris from other parts of Europe, this section is for you.

TRAIN STATION OVERVIEW

There are seven mainline rail stations in Paris. I'll list all seven, with their general service area in brackets, but the first three are most pertinent for us because they are the ones most likely to welcome international travelers.

1. **Gare du Nord** (UK, Belgium, Netherlands & Germany)
2. **Gare de l'Est** (Luxembourg, Germany)
3. **Gare de Lyon** (Switzerland, Italy)

4. Gare Saint-Lazare (Normandy)
5. Gare de Bercy (Burgundy)
6. Gare d'Austerlitz (Central France, Pyrenees)
7. Gare Montparnasse (Brittany, Southwest France)

The Gare du Nord and the Gare de l'Est are within roughly a 10min walk from one another and are located in the northeast area of Paris. The Gare de Lyon is located in the southeast.

AFTER ARRIVAL

Once you've arrived by train for your Paris vacation the best way to move out from the train station is by metro. Each mainline rail station will have several ticket booths where you'll be able to purchase regular metro tickets and **Mobilis** or **Paris Visite** passes (more about these in chapter five).

Depending on your arrival time, you could be faced with significant lineups to purchase your metro tickets. The inconvenience of lineups is compounded by the fact that many arriving are travel-weary and not all will speak French. If you don't speak fluent French, don't panic. Most service providers and staff are accustomed to working with international travelers and will have at least basic English.

That being said, it never hurts to begin any interaction with either "Bonjour Monsieur" or "Bonjour Madame", even if you're not able to continue in French after that. Think of it as the first step in getting on their good side (and you want to be on their good side). If you show overt disrespect or impatience, you can easily turn them off and will find them to be much less accommodating.

GENERAL TIPS

Tip #1: Do not purchase metro tickets from individuals in or around the station. Always use the authorized ticket window.

It is increasingly common to see automatic ticket machines

as well. For these, you will need either a chip-enabled bank card and or a card with a PIN number.

Tip #2: The metro is usually located one or two levels underground, so be prepared to navigate either escalators or stairs with any luggage.

Tip #3: For those *Starbucks* lovers among you, you'll be able to get your fix in the three main stations mentioned above.

Tip #4: If possible, avoid getting a hotel in close proximity to the train stations unless you absolutely have to or unless you've reserved ahead of time with a recognizable chain. I don't offer this tip out of a concern for safety but for cost. If you arrive on the spot looking for a room, you may find yourself paying top dollar for something little more than a large walk-in closet (by North American standards). Trust me, I speak from experience.

One thing that helps here is that most hotels will have their rates posted outside so that, before even going in, you'll have an idea of what cost you may be facing.

Section 4:
Luggage Storage

What if you have an early arrival in Paris, but you can't gain access to your accommodations until mid-late afternoon?

First of all, know that some of the chain hotels, if that's your accommodation of choice, *may* be able to hold them for you until check-in. This may not be the case with smaller, independent hotels however, as space is at a premium and large spacious lobbies are less common.

If you hotel is unable to story luggage for you or if, for

example, you are staying at an Airbnb, you'll need to come up with another option so you don't find yourself visiting the city with your suitcase in tow.

Let me give you a few options. **Note** that these are not endorsements as I've never had to use any of the services mentioned, but I offer them as possible solutions to the luggage storage problem.

Option #1 – Train Stations

Whether or not you have arrived by train, know that there are baggage storage services in many of the major mainline train stations in France. Gare du Nord is not exception. They offer luggage storage services from 6:15am to 11:15pm for a cost of 5€50 – 9€50, for the first 24 hours, depending on bag size.

If you are in the train station and looking for this service, you'll see it indicated as "Consignes automatiques / Left Luggage"

For more information on
luggage storage at train stations:
www.gares-sncf.com and search for "consignes bagages"

Option #2 – Nanny Bag

This is a web-based service that works with a network of hotels, shops and businesses who have space enough to temporarily store your bags.

Via www.NannyBag.com you choose your drop-off time, choose an available location and book your reservation online. You'll then receive an email confirmation with the exact address and details of your *bag nanny*.

Note that not all Nanny Bag partners are open 24hrs/day, you'll be limited by their hours of operation.

Option #3 – City Locker

www.CityLocker.fr is the web front-end for another network of storage locker facilities located throughout the city (often in, but not limited to, RER and metro stations) where you can leave your bags between 8am and 10pm, for a cost of 7€ - 16€, depending on locker size.

Once you make your online reservation, you will be sent, either by email or text message, an access code *(a)* to the storage locker facility and *(b)* for your assigned locker.

The one caution I would offer here is a reminder that you are reserving a specifically sized locker. If you get onsite and your measurements are off and the suitcase doesn't fit, there may or may not be staff onsite to help you resolve the issue without going back through the web-service.

DEPARTURE ACCOMMODATIONS

While we've barely just begun, I do want to touch on accommodations for your departure while still in the "at the airport" section of the book.

If you have a morning departure and would like to do everything possible to minimize disruptions or surprises, I'd recommend staying at the **Ibis Styles Roissypole**. By booking far enough in advance, you'll find very reasonable rates (70-80€/night) and this includes breakfast which is not the case in many airport hotels where you can pay up to 10€ for your morning meal. This Ibis Styles is a new property, is very clean and is only a 4min walk from the RER B and CDGVAL station.

IF you plan on staying there, let me again underscore the importance of booking ahead. I once found myself having to do a last minute departure and the lowest room available, among all airport hotels, was over 300€/night.

2

RESTAURANTS

My purpose in this chapter is not to give you a list of Parisian restaurants, for that alone would fill a library. Rather I want to give you a heads' up to some of the ways in which dining is different in France than in many other parts of the world; to help you know what you can expect.

At the end of the chapter I'll give you a couple of my personal favorites as places to begin.

WHAT'S YOUR TASTE?

There are two ways to think about food when in Paris.

If you want to see the city but still enjoy the comfort of the familiar, then you can easily find something that will fit the North American palette: Steaks, burgers & fries, omelets are all fairly standard fare in many restaurants.

If, on the other hand, you want to venture a bit further outside of your culinary comfort zone, then by all means, Paris is the place to do it. The French pride themselves on a rich history of great cuisine and you will surely not be disappointed. What's more, with so many ethnicities represented in Paris, each with their own unique cuisine, your options are just about endless.

WHAT IS FRENCH CUISINE?

Perhaps it'd be easier to make a choice on what you're looking for if I spelled out a bit more what the French dining experience consists of.

Menu Items

It's possible that what you most imagine French cuisine to be is determined by some of the more stereotypical dishes like escargots (snails) or foie gras. Know, however, that you'll find many of the same foods here on a French menu as you'd find at home. If your preference is for beef, lamb or poultry… you'll find it here as well. Although if home for you is Australia or Scotland, you may have trouble finding some of your more stereotypical dishes like crocodile, kangaroo or haggis.

Portion size and Preparation

While many of the basic elements might be familiar, two things that make a dish quite French are the portion size and the preparation.

In many restaurants, portion sizes will often seem very small by North American standards. This being said, the French are notorious for preferring quality over quantity. Remember too, that the French tend to eat their dinner in several courses.

In addition to portion size, preparation and presentation of the food is very important. Even when ordering a hamburger, for example, it's not uncommon to be asked how you'd like it cooked: saignant (rare), à point (medium) or bien cuit (well done) : not the case for fast food restaurants of course. You'll also often see rich sauces used both to complement the flavor and adorn the plate.

Aesthetic or appearance is very important to the French, from the way they carry themselves to the way they dress, etc. For this reason, your meal will be presented on the plate in a manner that is very appealing and attractive. Take time to admire the presentation before digging in. It's part of the experience.

Get-the-feeling tip:

The French certainly live by the expression
*"On mange avec les yeux avant de
manger avec la bouche."*

"We eat with our eyes before
we eat with our mouth."

Presentation is very important to the French.

The Experience

The final key to experiencing a truly French meal is to realize that your meal doesn't always have to be rushed. It is not uncommon for a meal to last for one to two hours because the emphasis is placed on being together, discussing and exchanging, rather than simply on eating and moving on to the next thing on the agenda.

I can't speak for other cultures, but particularly if you're from North America (as I am), you'll know that we can sometimes struggle with long dinners and can be a bit more prone to "eat and run."

Obviously, if you're on a three-day trip to Paris, you might not want all your meals to be long ones, but you owe it to yourself to enjoy at least one slow meal, spread out over several courses.

Paris has no lack of restaurants to help you do that, but if you'd like to combine such a meal with unparalleled views, you'll find my recommendation for a dinner cruise in chapter eight.

GENERAL TIPS

Tip #1: Menu or à-la-Carte?

There's a difference between how English uses the word **menu** and how French uses it.

In France, *un menu* is a fixed-price meal which, depending on what you select, may or may not include dessert, coffee, an appetizer, etc. You usually get a good bang for your buck but choosing a menu.

The typical English use of the word menu (to select from all items on the "menu") is expressed in French with the term "à la carte" (literally "off the menu"). You'll have a wider choice in what you can order but the average price of the entire meal will generally be higher. (I'll give you a tip for reducing your overall bill in chapter eight.)

Tip #2: Tipping

Unlike in North America where tipping a minimum of 15-20% is customary, know that you do not need to leave a tip at French restaurants as a rule and if you choose not to, it's not considered rude.

Most times, the service is included in the price of your meal and servers' wages are higher than in North America. That being said, if you've had particularly good service, no server will ever refuse a few extra Euros, but again, well below the 15-20% North American norm.

Tip #3: Leftovers and Sharing

If you're traveling from North America, two fairly common things are much less common in Europe and especially in Paris: Sharing dishes and doggy bags for leftovers.

> **Sharing:** Consider pizza for example. In North America it would be common to order a single pizza for 2-4 people or more. That is less done here and while it may be permitted in some restaurants (primarily outside of the capital) it is up to the discretion of the restaurant manager and is not the standard practice by default.
>
> **Doggy Bags:** Similarly, while it can be common in North America and other places to request a doggy bag in which to carry away any uneaten portion of your meal, know that it is less common in Parisian restaurants. One thing that works against the practice is, as mentioned above, portion sizes tend to be smaller and less bolstered by carbohydrates like

French fries, potatoes, etc. You can always ask (I typically wouldn't), but don't be surprised if it is not possible.

Tip #4: Gluten Free and Food Intolerances

If you are traveling to Paris and come with various food allergies, you should keep a few things in mind.

Grocery Stores: Most of the grocery stores stock items that are gluten free and are labeled *"sans gluten."* In the city however, you likely won't be visiting the large supermarkets, but you may find yourself passing smaller ones like Franprix, Monoprix, Carrefour Market, etc.

Restaurants: If you will encounter difficulty anywhere, it may be in restaurants that don't cater exclusively to a gluten free or other food intolerant clientele. Some servers may be unaware of which items are gluten free and others may be have the idea that a customer requesting gluten free is simply participating in a dietary trend, not fully appreciating or understanding the health complications involved.

If you're looking for help finding gluten free friendly restaurants, sites like **TheFork.com** and **Yelp** can help you find establishments that have declared themselves to have gluten free options.

In short, finding restaurants that plan for gluten free or allergen sensitive guests likely won't be as easy in Paris as it may be elsewhere, but it is not impossible. If there is some way of having written, in French, exactly what your allergies or intolerances are, it would not be a bad idea to have something like that with you.

PERSONAL FAVOURITES

Here are a few of my favorite food stops in Paris:

L'Entracte

1 rue Auber

(9th arrondissement, metro: Opera)

Just steps away from and in full view of the Opéra Garnier, you'll find fast service and croque monsieurs or omelets, fries & salad as well as other standard brasserie fare for as little as 14-17€/person.

La Boussole:

12 rue Guisarde

(6th arrondissement, metro: Mabillon)

This restaurant is only a short walk from the legendary Boulevard Saint Germain.

www.la-boussole.com

Chez Clément:

123 avenue des Champs Élysées

(8th arrondissement, metro: Georges V)

Incredible service, great menu. There are several locations around the city, but this one puts you just steps from the Arc de Triomphe.

Factory & Co.:

23 Cour Saint Émilion

(12th arrondissement, Metro: Cour Saint Emilion)

There are several places to dine in the Cour Saint-Émilion but this one is unique. Hearty sandwiches on bagels with street-level dining or, if you prefer, lower-level dining in what was once a wine cellar. Finish off your meal with one of their to-die-for cheesecakes.

www.factoryandco.com/les-restaurants/bercy-village

Latin Quarter:

> (Opposite Notre Dame
>
> Metro: St-Michel Notre Dame)
>
> In these pedestrian streets there are plenty of sit-down restaurants, but if you're eating on the go or preparing a quick quai-side picnic, grab a gyro on rue de la Huchette and follow up with some sweet treats from Sud Tunisien at the bottom of rue de la Harpe.

Berthillon:

> (Île Saint-Louis at the end of the Saint-Louis bridge, behind Notre Dame)
>
> In addition to a beautiful terrace with views of Notre Dame, you'll also find a great selection of Italian-style homemade ice cream. Over and above the traditional flavors, why not try some of their unique blends such as Grilled Pineapple & Basil, Gooseberry, Apricot, Spiced Bread or Hazelnut. All this homemade goodness doesn't come cheap: one scoop is 3€50, two scoops are 6€50 and a triple scoop will run you 9€… but no one's saying you can't share or, if you're traveling alone, indulge.

La Charlotte de l'Île:

> 24 Rue Saint-Louis en l'Île, Île Saint-Louis
>
> (4th Arrondissement, Metro: Cité or Sully-Morland)
>
> More than just their hot chocolate à l'ancienne, you can coffee with their out-of-this-world lemon tarts.

You may or may not even see any of the restaurants that I've mentioned here, but if not, no worries, Once again, there is simply no shortage of incredible dining experiences waiting for you in Paris.

3

ACCOMMODATIONS

There are thousands of accommodation choices in Paris and your choice will be based on a number of factors:

- Level of comfort
- Cost
- Location (proximity to sights)
- Ease of access
- Brand recognition or loyalty programs
- Etc.

Because of this, as was the case with the previous chapter, rather than attempting to build a directory of hotel choices, I will limit the scope of this chapter and offer instead an overview of a few brands that may be unfamiliar to non-European travelers.

It's worth noting that room sizes will typically be smaller than what would be common in North America. As a mega-city, space is limited and comes at a premium.

BUDGET BRANDS

Below are a few brands that are common in France, but which may be unfamiliar if you are coming from away.

Ibis Hotels

Ibis hotels are part of the Accor Group and have several brands:

Ibis Budget:

By reserving online, you can get rooms in the 45-50€ range under certain conditions. My experience has been positive I've had clean rooms and dealt with pleasant staff. There will be virtually no sitting area in the rooms and breakfast is not included, though it can be added on for 9-10€ per person. You pretty much just get a bed & bathroom, but if this is your price range and you're merely looking for a place to lay your head at night, this will fit the bill.

Ibis:

This is a step up from the Ibis Budget and you'll find the prices more in the 80-100€ range. Again, breakfast is typically not included.

Ibis Styles:

This is my preferred brand of the three. Rooms are between 100-130€ per night, however breakfast is included and there is typically a little more space.

Kyriad Hotels

This is another economical chain that I've used in Paris. The rooms are clean and, while the rooms are fairly small (again, simply because it's Paris) it's a great budget option.

Independent Hotels

You will also come across many independent hotels tucked in between cafés, businesses or personal residences. While it's impossible to guide you in any meaningful way on individual properties, there are a couple of things that will help you make a reasonable guess-timation as to whether or not you might want to stay at a given location.

Tip #1: Most hotels in France post their pricing structure outside at the entrance of the building. This allows you an idea of what rate to expect (whether specific prices or rate ranges) and whether or not breakfast is included (*petit-déjeuner inclus*).

Tip #2: If you are preplanning your trip, check out sites like **Tripadvisor** or **Yelp** to see what kind of reviews a particular property has received. If you are planning on-the-go then you can still check out these sites on your smartphone, but simply be sure about your data allowance and any roaming charges.

MID-UPPER RANGE BRANDS

In the three to four-star range of accommodations in Paris, you'll find **Novotel** and **Mercure** chains. The **Sofitel** and **Pullman** hotels are on the upper end of that scale.

WORLD-WIDE BRANDS

If you belong to the loyalty programs of some of the world-wide brands (Best Western, Radisson, Hilton, Marriott, etc) you will, of course find properties in Paris by perusing the your normal reservation portals.

AIRBNB

I've placed Airbnb in its own category because you can find Paris rentals in all price brackets.

If you're not familiar with Airbnb, this web platform offers the possibility of staying in the home of local residents; renting a single room (with the owners still present) or an entire apartment (where the owners are absent).

We've stayed in a studio in the 50€/night range, but prices vary according to size and location. Here are two things to keep in mind when choosing an Airbnb location:

> **Proximity to Metro / RER lines:** If you're out late and miss the last metro, it could be a long walk / taxi ride back. Missing the last metro is not difficult to do in some areas, particularly in summer when darkness only falls near 10:30-11:00pm. You stay out a little past dark, to see the Eiffel Tower lit up and before you know it, it's past midnight.

> **Location of the accommodation *in* the building:** If your apartment is on the 7th or 8th floor, for example, you could well be faced with a winding staircase or a tiny elevator. By "tiny" I mean, "two people and one small suitcase will be a tight squeeze." This isn't meant to be a deterrent, simply a heads up of what you might encounter.

BOOKING

In today's online world, you can either book directly with a particular hotel via their website or you can go through a platform such as Booking.com.

There are enough options to ensure that accommodation need not be a particularly daunting or outrageously pricey thing, unless of course that's not a concern for you.

It goes without saying that anything booked through a regular worldwide chain comes with the comfort of familiarity, but the chains I've mentioned are all reputable.

With any kind of private rental situation (Airbnb for example) you simply need to adopt a buyer-beware approach to all aspects of the process. Due diligence is time well spent and can go a long way to minimizing problems in the long run.

MIKE LONG

4

BE PARISIAN

Remember *the feeling* I talked about in the "Why I Wrote this Book" section? One of the ways you can cultivate that feeling is to understand a few things that come naturally to native Parisians. Another way is to try to live like one of them... if only on a limited scale and for a limited time. That's what this chapter is all about.

SECTION 1: TERMINOLOGY

There are a few terms that will help you navigate your way through Paris or will at least help when people direct you to certain areas.

Rive Gauche – Rive Droite

The Seine River snakes through the city from east to west, cutting the city in two. Everything south of the Seine is referred to as being *Rive Gauche* (Left Bank). For example:

The Assemblée Nationale (National Assembly – the French Parliament), the Latin Quarter and the Eiffel Tower are all south of the Seine and are referred to as being *Rive Gauche*.

The Louvre, l'Hôtel de Ville (City Hall) and the Opéra Garnier are all north of the Seine. Consequently, they are not referred to as being *Rive Gauche*, rather, they are situated *Rive Droite*.

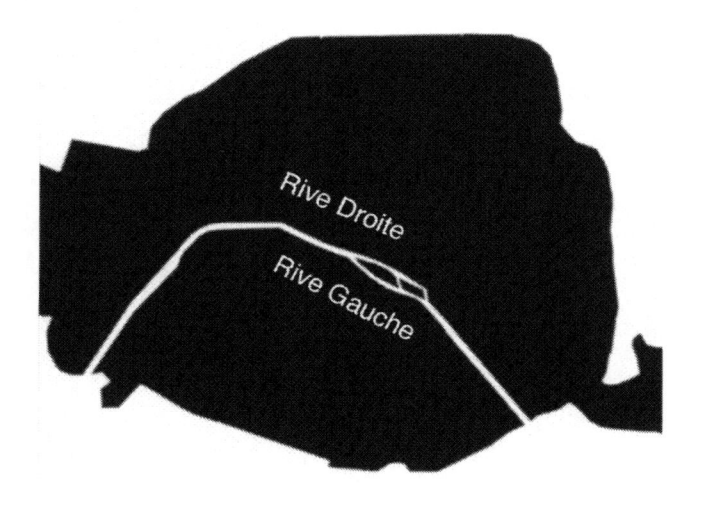

La Bise *(pronounced: La BEEZ)*

This is how the French greet one another, by touching cheeks and making the kissing sound. Shoot for the left side first followed by the right side.

Most commonly, it is done between women or between men and women. Generally speaking, it is only done between men when they are already very good friends or family. When in doubt… let the French lead the way and follow their lead.

Arrondissements

The closest English equivalent to the French term *arrondissement* is "borough" or perhaps, in a very broad sense, neighborhood. It denotes a geographic administration district of the city.

There are 20 arrondissements in Paris and the term is used extensively to situate businesses, restaurants, sights, etc. The lower the number, the closer the arrondissement is to the center of Paris and they spiral clockwise and outward from the center.

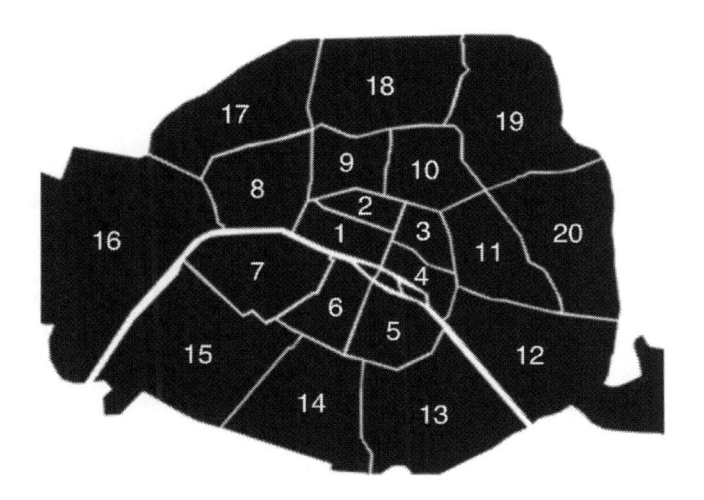

Study up on the general location of the various arrondissements below and you'll impress even the most well-established Parisian.

Quai

Technically, the French word *quai* refers to a dock and is reminiscent of the days when riverboats would dock almost anywhere along the river to unload their wares.

Docking areas were eventually named individually, which is why, in the vicinity of Notre Dame you will find that the same riverside stretch of road will have different names, according to where you are located.

Within a five-minute walk of Notre Dame there are no fewer than six quais. The first four are situated Rive Gauche while numbers five and six are located on Île de la Cité:

1. Quai de Montebello
2. Quai Saint-Michel
3. Quai des Grands Augustins
4. Quai de la Tournelle
5. Quai du Marché Neuf
6. Quai des Orfèvres

Note that 36 Quai des Orfèvres is where Paris' Prefecture of Police is located. Not only did it lend its name to a 1947 film, but in 2014 a thief stole 52kg (114lbs) of cocaine right from under the police's nose. The drug had been seized after a long investigation and was key evidence for the eventual trial. As it turns out, a 2017 trial convicted one of the police's own employees who worked on the premises, with the theft. Sounds like a story straight out of a whodunit film crossed with a good cop-bad cop reel.

The clincher: the ex-police officer apparently did the deed

by smuggling the drug out in reusable shopping bags. Want a neat picture? Have someone snap a photo of you, along the Quai des Orfèvres with a heavy-laden shopping bag and weave your own tale of intrigue from there.

Back to the Quais...

When we speak of a *quai* in general, without naming any one in particular, it refers no only to the street-level sidewalk area but also to the pedestrian areas located directly at water-level. These are surprisingly open and accessible given the amount of boat traffic that travels the Seine.

During the daytime, many come to the *quais* to eat a quick lunch away from the hubbub of the streets. In the evening, however, the *quais* are overflowing with life as many locals bring a bottle of wine and something to eat, whether to celebrate a special occasion with friends or just enjoy the out of doors. It is not uncommon for impromptu music concerts to pop up in the hopes of gaining a bit of spare change from tourists or selling CDs. Some "concerts" however are simply a question of musician friends getting together to jam for the fun of it.

> ### *Get-the-feeling tip:*
>
> The *quais* are a wonderful place to stroll and a quintessential part of the Parisian experience. The emphasis here is on the word *"stroll"* ... take your time; breathe, experience and enjoy.
>
> If by chance you are a runner, the *quais* make a great place to run as well. You'll deal with less traffic than at street level.

Sympa

This is a shortened form of *sympathique* or nice (not related semantically to the English: sympathetic). It's a way of expressing appreciation for something without going overboard. For example:

> "How'd you like that new restaurant?"
> "Bien, c'était sympa."

Bonjour Madame / Bonsoir Monsieur

I alluded to this in chapter one, but one of the things that differentiates French culture from my home culture (North American) is the way that we approach people.

If I was home and looking for assistance in a store, I'd simply say "Excuse me…" or "Hello…" and launch directly into my question. The subtle difference in France is that people tend to formally acknowledge one another with a "Bonjour Madame (Good day ma'am) or a "Bonsoir Monsieur." (Good evening sir) before launching into a question or requesting information.

More than simply *Bonjour* or *Bonsoir*, the addition of *Monsieur* or *Madame* communicates just that extra bit of formal respect that is both part of French culture and appreciated by the French.

It's a subtle difference, but a simple way to be just a little bit more French.

SECTION 2: ACTIVITIES

Below is a list of sixteen things you can easily include as part of your time in Paris. They are quick and, for the most part, inexpensive yet they're guaranteed to add that certain "je ne sais quoi" to your visit and will send you home boasting of becoming nigh unto a real Parisian!

(Note: this is a "Get-the-Feeling Tip" goldmine!)

1. Picnic along the Seine

Grab a jambon-beurre sandwich (ham & butter), a Perrier, a *pain-au-chocolat* and head down to picnic on one of the quais along the Seine. Want to add a flair of the exotic? If you're in the vicinity of the Saint-Michel area, grab a Tunisian pastry at Sud Tunisien.

2. Sidewalk Bistro

Have coffee at a sidewalk café, even in winter. Regardless of the season, if dressed for the weather then you're ready for the ultimate people-watching experience. Grab a seat at one of the countless bistro terraces and sip your café-au-lait very leisurely as the world passes you by.

Note that in cooler weather, bistros often have outside heating above the tables making it more comfortable than one might think.

3. Late Dining

Be prepared to dine later than you perhaps would at home. Many restaurants don't even open their doors until 7:00pm.

4. Guys... Scarf-up!

Buy and wear a scarf. They're sold according to season in order to keep the breeze off your neck (and because it's French chic). Even in summer, you'll find very lightweight linen scarves. You can usually track some down in the metro shopping areas, in the souvenir shops and at some of the train stations for 5-6€.

Instructions for wearing it like the French.

- Fold the scarf in half length-wise
- Wrap the folded scarf around your neck
- Pass the two ends through the loop and...
- Voilà... French chic!

5. Ladies... Accessorize!

The easiest way is to purchase a scarf or a *foulard*, like the guys, but you have many other ways to wear it. Again, they are inexpensive and come in many prints, fabrics and budgets. You can easily find something for less than 10€ in all major souvenir areas, train stations and regular shops.

6. Wear Sunglasses

Anytime is sunglasses time, regardless of the weather; summer, winter, rain or shine! That certain *je-ne-sais-quoi* is easily achieved by donning shades.

7. Stay in micro-accommodations

I mention this in chapter three but living in a tiny space is a common Parisian experience. Give it a go, if only for a night or two. It'll give you bragging rights (if it doesn't give you a crick in the neck!).

8. Ditch the tights, sweats & runners

… unless you're exercising.

OK, this might be pushing it, but you rarely see Parisians in exercise clothing unless they're on their way to, or returning from, a workout. They are *chic* personified, so if aerobic-friendly makes up your normal travel wardrobe, take at least one day's worth of comfy chic (without forgetting #7 above), preferably in black or grey, with the splash of color afforded by a foulard (see #5 above).

9. Exercise at the foot of Lady Liberty

If you *do* want to include some exercise and your accommodation has no provision for that, no problem. Beneath the bridge adjacent to the Statue of Liberty, you will find a full workout facility, right in the good old outdoors. It's free of charge but is a bit off the beaten track. The Statue of Liberty stands at the end of l'Île aux Cygnes, just west of the Eiffel Tower, on the Seine River.

10. Riverside Dancing

There are four open-air amphitheatres along the Quai Saint-Bernard (just south of Notre Dame) that come alive nightly to the sounds of Salsa, Tango, Swing and Folk music during the summer. Spectators need not be intimidated, you may even find someone offering free lessons.

11. "French" French Fries

In many parts of the world, ketchup is the sauce of choice when it comes to an order of fries. In France, however, a good many people opt for mayonnaise in stead. Give it a try or, for a real twist, mix mayonnaise with your ketchup.

12 Try Sushi

You may be shaking your head at this one, but sushi has become somewhat of an obsession with the French in recent years.

13. Get out of Tourist-Ville

You don't need to go far and you don't need to stay long, but you can experience the less touristy side of Paris by taking the metro away from the center and out toward the *périphérique* (ring road surrounding the city). I'd suggest taking the metro's #4 line out to the Alésia stop. Once above ground, stroll the streets, grab a bite to eat or simply enjoy *un p'tit café*. Don't worry though, if you're feeling too much like a fish out of water, there's still a Starbucks within two minutes of the metro.

14. Slow Down

The only people rushing around Paris are the tourists and the people who are late for work. Parisians have mastered the art of strolling (in French they call it "flâner"). So while here, throw on your sunglasses (#6), don your French chic (#8) and stroll through one of the many covered shopping streets – even if you have no intention of buying. Then, find a nice little sidewalk bistro (#2) and spend some time people watching. For an evening stroll, head down to the quais to watch others stroll as the Bateaux Mouches pass.

15. Books

The French are great readers and it's not uncommon for them to have a book out while on the metro, while sitting at a café table or lounging on a park bench. France's staunch literary heritage is reinforced on book and one reader at a time. If you didn't bring one with you, purchase one from the Bouquinistes (green boxes along the Seine) or from one of the many bookstores south of the Seine, Rive Gauche.

16. Go Sailing Kids (or kids at heart)

In both the Luxembourg Gardens and the Tuilleries Gardens you can sail a toy sailboat in the fountain for a couple of Euros. Go one… you know you want to!

MIKE LONG

5

GETTING AROUND

Once you're in Paris, there are a few ways to get from one point of interest to another and different ways to discover the city. In this chapter, besides the metro system – the most obvious choice – I'll also give you three other options.

METRO

The Paris metro is the very best way to explore the entire city quickly and at a reasonable cost. While individual tickets are available for only 1€80, and purchasing them in books of 10 allows you to get them for a little more than 1€40 each, there is an even better solution for a 2-3 day stay.

Paris Visite Card

Paris' transport authority, the RATP, has partnered with a number of monuments, museums and other tour operators to come up with the Paris Visite card. It gives you unlimited travel on the metro, RER lines, city buses and even the Montmartre funicular. Not only that, but presentation of the pass will afford you a number of discounts at various museums and points of interest, including the famed Galleries Lafayette department store.

You'll choose your pass based primarily on two factors:

1. The duration of your pass in number of days
2. The zones within which you'd like to travel (Are you staying downtown or going further out?)

For a short visit, zones 1-3 will suffice. A pass allowing you to travel in zones 1-5 would only be necessary if you wanted to visit Versailles, Disneyland Paris or the airports for example.

For **zones 1-3**, a 2-day pass (18,95€) or a 3-day pass (25,85€) will give you total liberty within the downtown core. It gives you maximum flexibility in addition to all the extra perks and discounts.

> **Note:** prior to using the card for the first time, you need to write your full name as well as the dates of intended use on the card. Without this, your card will not be considered valid and could earn you a fine.

You can purchase Paris Visite card at all metro windows.

For more information:
www.ratp.fr/en and search for "paris visite"

PARIS 3 DAYS NO STRESS: A Travel Guide

MOBILIS Card

If you'd like almost all of the flexibility of the Paris Visite card but don't think you'll need all of the extras, the Mobilis card is an option for you. When I know I'm going to be doing a lot of running around in Paris, on a single day, I'll often go this route.

Mobilis gives you unlimited travel in the metro and for a slightly lower cost than the Paris Visite card (like Paris Visite, it is priced according to travel zones). Where a one day Paris Visite pass, for zones 1-3, costs 11,65€, a Mobilis card for the same duration and same travel area is 9,70€.

Similar to the Paris Visite card, you must indicate your full name and dates of use on the card prior to using it for the first time and it can be purchased at metro ticket windows. Just remember that the Mobilis pass does not give the other perks or discounts afforded by Paris Visite.

For more information on
the <i>Mobilis</i> card see:
www.ratp.fr/en and search for "mobilis"

(Note: there is no English translation of Mobilis Card info because it is more intended for locals and not tourists)

Get-the-feeling tip:

When nearing the exit of many metro stations, you'll feel the wind hit your face (warm in summer & cool in the winter). Be aware of the sensation. It's like Paris giving you "la bise" each time you resurface.

I suggest downloading a map of the metro to your smart phone. It's more discreet than pulling out a map and you'll have the information at your fingertips. Search for **RATP Paris Metro Map** in your normal app store.

VELIB'

There's something awfully romantic about being able to say that you've bicycled your way around Paris. Fortunately, it's quite doable thanks to Velib', a self-service bike system that has over 26,000 bikes available at over 1,800 bike stations throughout the city. Not only is it romantic or nostalgic, but it's also a very eco-friendly way to visit the French capital.

Cost

It's possible to do it very inexpensively as the first ½ hour is always free. If you'd like to be able to say you've done it and then return your bike within the first 30 minutes, you'll have paid nothing. Be careful though, the rate quickly goes up for each following ½ hour increment. (My daughter and I once went biking and ended up paying 7€ each for a 1.5hr ride.)

To simply show up at the bike station and purchase your first ticket is doable, but is a bit of a process. You've got to provide a credit card and Velib' will put a 150€ hold on your account (just in case a user doesn't return the bike), but the hold will be cancelled upon return of the bike.

It is not a very straightforward process and you will need a dose of patience, particularly since, if you just show up to the station, there is no attending personnel and you have to work on an LED screen roughly the size of a cell phone. If I had it to do again, I'd pre-purchase a 1-day pass on the company's website (en.velib.paris.fr) for only 1€70. My understanding is that you will still have to pay regular tariffs, but it eliminates the need to work through the user agreements, etc. on the bike station screen. In stead, you do the legwork at ease, from the comfort of your own home and on a computer screen or tablet. This way, the initial rental process becomes much easier.

Where to Bike?

If you're completely without fear and have a great sense of direction (or a good map), then pretty much the whole city is ready to be discovered. Just beware of traffic. While Parisians are used to sharing the road with bikes, they remain very aggressive drivers and this can be intimidating.

If you're looking for a tamer bike experience then the following areas might be of interest to you.

- A number of **main through-fares** do have bike lanes, but the adjacent car traffic will be heavy at times.

- There is a wide pedestrian area that runs along much of the Rive Gauche (south of the Seine) between the Assemblée Nationale and the Eiffel Tower, the **Promenade des Berges de la Seine André Gorz** (see map below).

- The area surrounding the Louvre and the Tuilleries Gardens are bike accessible although – and this is important – bikes are **not** permitted inside the Tuilleries Gardens themselves.

- There are some wide pedestrian areas leading up part of the **Champs Élysées** that make for a stretch of fairly relaxed biking.

- Large parks such as the **Champs de Mars** (Eiffel Tower) and the **Esplanade des Invalides** are both fairly open and make great backdrops for photos. (note that some parts of these parks may not be open to bike traffic. Always keep your eye open for signage prohibiting bikes in a given area)

- **L'Île aux Cygnes** (Swan Island) is a long and very narrow island leading from the Bir-Hakeim bridge down to the Statue of Liberty. There is no car traffic and only foot traffic to compete with. It makes for a beautiful bike ride, again with views of both the Eiffel Tower and the Statue of Liberty as backdrops for some great photos of you and your bike!

- Both the **Bois de Boulogne** and the **Bois de Vincennes** are large parks with lots of room to bike. Although I wouldn't recommend the Bois de Boulogne after nightfall. As always watch for signage in some areas of these large parks.

Below you'll find a map with these suggestions and more, 10 in total, for fairly relaxed biking around Paris.

If you're not too sure about venturing too far around the city, that's understandable. Paris is big and there are some very heavy traffic areas. Still though, with a little pre-planning, there's definitely a way to enjoy some biking in a way, and in areas, that are quite relaxing and low on traffic.

Returning your Velib

Be sure, when returning our bike, that it "clicks in" to the bike stand properly. Otherwise, your bike will not be considered "returned", someone could potentially come behind you a take the bike, in which case you would lose the 150€ deposit being held on your credit card.

PARIS 3 DAYS NO STRESS: A Travel Guide

If you have trouble returning the bike, each station has a speaker-phone connection to the office. They may be able to walk you through any difficulty, providing you have the reference number from on your rental ticket.

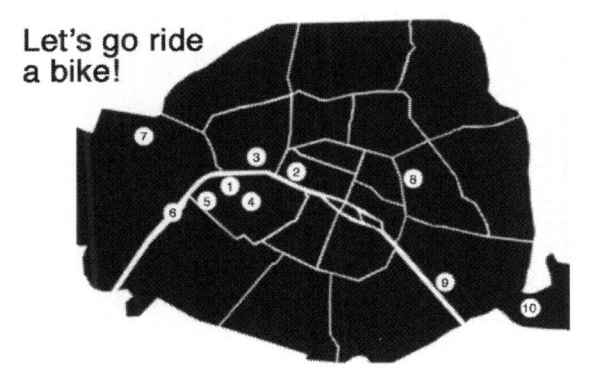

Let's go ride a bike!

1. **Assemblée National to the Eiffel Tower:** Promenade des Berges de la Seine André Gorz
2. **Tuilleries Gardens** *(around the raised perimeter only, NOT inside the park)*
3. **Avenue des Champs Élysées**
4. **Around the Esplanade des Invalides and up the Avenue de Breteuil**
5. **Parc du Champ de Mars** *(some areas & paths are off limits to bikes)*
6. **Île aux Cygnes** *(Between the Pont Bir Hakeim and the Pont de la Grenelle)*
7. **Bois de Boulogne** *(From the Arc de Triomphe via Avenue Foch - avoid at night)*
8. **Boulevard Richard Lenoir to Canal Saint-Martin**
9. **Along the Quais to the Parc de Bercy** *(Bikes not permitted IN the park)*
10. **Bois de Vincennes** *(Watch signage, some areas are for horses only)*

Always watch for and obey signage!
Tourists are not exempt from ticketing by police for biking
in areas where signage clearly prohibits it.

BATOBUS

For an alternative to taxi, bus or metro, you do have the option of moving around Paris using the BatoBus service, essentially a water-taxi service that stops at nine different stations along the downtown portion of the Seine River.

Tickets aren't particularly inexpensive at 17€ per person, for a full-day pass (8€ for children), but you do have the double advantage of seeing many of the principal monuments from the river as well as avoiding the crowded tunnels of the metro.

Unlike the sightseeing cruises, however, there is no running commentary on the nearby sights or monuments, however it allows you to hop on and hop off as many times as you like, offers a slower paced alternative and provides lots of opportunities for photos.

Stop stations are located at:

1. Eiffel Tower (7th arrond.)
2. Musée d'Orsay (7th arrond.)
3. Saint-Germain-des-Près (5th arrond.)
4. Notre Dame (4th arrond.)
5. Jardin des Plantes /
   Cité de la Mode et du Design (5th arrond.)
6. Hôtel de Ville (4th arrond.)
7. Louvre (1st arrond.)
8. Champs Élysées (8th arrond.)
9. Beaugrenelle (15th arrond.)
   (near the Statue of Liberty)

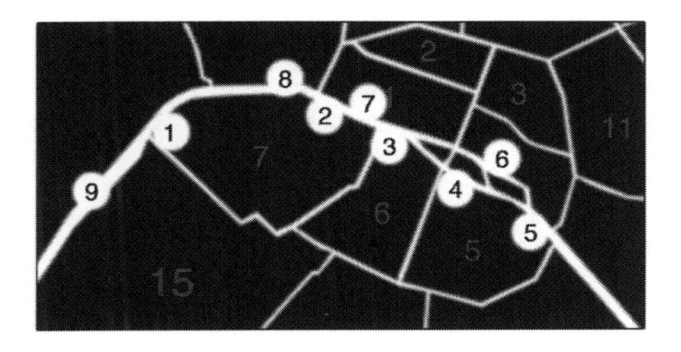

You can see from this list, that one could easily visit many of the principal downtown attractions by purchasing a BatoBus day-pass. This is a particularly great alternative if you are slightly intimidated by the idea of navigating the metro system.

It's Worth Noting:

- The timing of boats varies according to season. They can be as close as every 25 minutes during high-tourist months and down to every 40 minutes in slower seasons.

- There will be stairs to navigate if you use the BatoBus service. Stop stations are located at quai-side, but the street-level is only accessible by stairs.

For more information on BatoBus
see www.BatoBus.com/en.html

HOP-ON / HOP-OFF BUS TOURS

Another way to see Paris from above ground is one of the Hop-on Hop-off, double decker bus tours of the city. Several companies offer this type of service and you can get a good overall view of tour offerings on their website (referenced below).

By way of introduction, let me say that there are tour packages for all budgets and with various add-ons, depending on whether you want to make your bus tour a simple add-on to your already mostly planned visit **or** whether you decide to make it your principal means of visiting the city.

For example, you can get a basic 24hr pass for as little at 18€ (though they speak of a 24hr pass, note that busses don't run 24hrs. They generally don't operate between late evening and the early morning – see below), giving you access to many of the downtown sights.

Alternatively, you can access a truly premium package with **The Paris Pass**, beginning at 127€ per person. This is a Cadillac of a product that gives you not only one day of hop-on hop-off bus access, but also includes:

- Free entry to over 65 museums and attractions
- Fast-track / skip the line access to some places
- A Paris event guide and city map
- A Paris-Visite pass and metro map
- Special offers or gifts at select locations.

It's Worth Noting:

- Most companies operate between 9:30am and 6-7:00pm (unless you purchase a night-tour package)
- Most provide audio commentary of sights.
- You can typically join or leave the tour at a location that is convenient for you.

For more information see
see www.hop-on-hop-off-bus.com

As you can see, there is no shortage of options for *how* you can visit Paris. They all provide quite a variety in terms of flexibility, pricing and convenience. For that reason, you'll easily be able to find a method that suits your preferred pace and comfort level.

That sums up the *how*… now let's look at the *what*: Nine of the major must-see sights and attractions that you don't want to miss.

MIKE LONG

6

WHAT TO DO

There are literally thousands of things that you could do during your stay in Paris, between museums, exhibits, shows and monuments. For your short stay however, I recommend that you consider at least including the following.

SIGHTSEEING CRUISES

Metro: Pont Neuf

Unless you're petrified of water, then a sightseeing cruise on the Seine River is a must-do during your stay in Paris.

The most well-known of all river cruise companies in Paris is by far Les Bateaux Mouches. That being said, I've never travelled with them, opting instead for the **Vedettes du Pont Neuf**, located not very far from Notre Dame at the end of the Île de la Cité. Cruises leave every ½ hour and are 1 hour in duration.

Planning ahead will allow you to reap a small reward in terms of ticket price. With Vedettes du Pont Neuf for example, if you purchase an "Open Ticket" online, you'll pay 10€ rather than the normal 14€ and tickets are good on all cruises, for the chosen date, subject to availability.

You can be sure of your seat by purchasing their "Advantage Ticket", which guarantees your seat for a preselected sailing time, but which will only save you 2€ as opposed to 4€ with the open ticket.

In my opinion, unless you are going at the absolute busiest time (July/August) you will find seats easily… go with the "Open Ticket."

Travelling with Fido? No problem. If you are travelling with your small or medium sized dog, he is welcome aboard the Vedettes du Pont Neuf boats as long as it remains on a leash. Smaller breads can be brought aboard either on a leash or in an appropriate purse or shoulder bag. Admission of larger or typically aggressive breeds may or may not be allowed.

For more information see
www.vedettesdupontneuf.com

(To avoid possible confusion, note that another company "Vedettes de Paris" exists and is located near the Eiffel Tower. These are two different companies.)

> ### *Get-the-feeling tip:*
>
> While you'll not get the same impression as in Titanic *(we hope!)*, there is something special about – if you're travelling with someone special – standing at the rail of one of these boat tours, the wind at your back while passing the Eiffel Tower.

Interested in a dinner cruise?
I'll give you my recommendation in chapter 8

Eiffel Tower

Metro: Trocadero (A)
Bir Hakeim (B)

Why am I giving you two possible metro stops? Because there are two ways of approaching the Eiffel Tower and each is spectacular in its own way.

Option A: metro Trocadero

Coming to the Eiffel Tower this way has the advantage of bringing you via the Trocadero Esplanade, which overlooks the Eiffel tower from a bit of a distance. You'll be able to take a selfie or a group-selfie (a groupie?) and have the entire tower in the background.

From there you'll walk down a number of stairs and sloping pathways through the Trocadero gardens and along the fountain, past the carousel at the base of the hill.

Between the esplanade and the park, you'll encounter many clandestine souvenir sellers. They're not dangerous and will be very willing to barter, so **don't** take their first offer.

Continuing on, you'll cross the Seine via the Pont d'Iéna, arriving at the foot of Paris' great "damme de fer" (iron lady), the spectacular Eiffel Tower.

At a leisurely pace, you can expect to walk for 10-15 minutes from Trocadero, your tower-views changing with each step.

Option B: metro Bir Hakeim

Arriving at the Eiffel Tower via the Bir Hakeim metro station will also require a 5-10 minute walk. The tower will be hidden from view for most of this walk, however it makes your first views all the more impressive as you arrive almost at the foot of the western pillar.

The Tower Itself

There are several ways of accessing the Eiffel Tower, but before you even get a chance to purchase tickets, you'll have to go through the security check. You will have to discard any sharp objects and present your bags for inspection.

You can purchase tickets upon arrival but you'll generally have to endure long lineups. There are **two options for minimizing your wait time:**

1. You can pre-purchase tickets online. You will definitely want to do this if you (a) want to visit

the top of the tower or (b) are travelling in a group. Note that 2-3 months ahead is not too soon to order your tickets and increase the chance of getting your first choice of visit times. Rates for adults are 11€ to the first and second floors and 17€ to the top.

2. There is always less wait time when you opt to take the stairs, as opposed to the elevator, up to the first level. It's less expensive as well, coming in at only 7€.

For more information on the Eiffel Tower
www.EiffelTower.paris/en

Caution: if young ladies approach you with a clipboard or paper in hand, inviting you to complete a survey, **avoid them;** they are typically pickpockets. It is common to see them in the Eiffel Tower area (whether around the base of the tower or at the Trocadero Esplanade). Security is typically not far away so you needn't be overly concerned, simply avoid engaging them in conversation.

Sacré Coeur - Montmartre

Metro: Anvers

Montmartre is quite a place but be forewarned, it's on the top of a hill so it will involve walking uphill.

Probably the most convenient metro stop is Anvers, as indicated above. When you come up out of the metro, you'll walk up rue Steinkerque, a street where you'll find tons of souvenir shops with very competitive pricing. I usually find that prices are 1-2€ lower here on many items, perhaps because it's just a bit more out of the way than rue Rivoli (near the Louvre).

> **Caution:** Along this street you may see people betting money on a "find-the-ball-under-one-of-the-three-cups" game of chance. Avoid them. The fact that they bolt when police are near should tell you something.

Reaching the Top

At the top of rue Steinkerque, you still have a bit of a hike to get up to Sacré Coeur, but you do have three options:

1. The **most direct way** to access Sacré Coeur is to take the winding stairs and pathways through the park at the base of the monument. You'll also have a chance to ride a Carousel if you choose. One is located at the foot of the hill.

2. The **least strenuous way** to access the church is to take the Montmartre Funicular, an slanted elevator of sorts. It takes less than two minutes to get to the top, it runs all day, and costs the same price as a metro ticket.

3. The **path less traveled** is a straight stairway immediately adjacent to the funicular, known as the rue Foyatier stairway. These 300 steps are not for the faint of heart. Unless you are willing to take your time, you'll find yourself quite out of

breath upon reaching the top. If you *do* take your time however, you will fully enjoy one of the most breathtaking and typically elegant stairway streets in Paris, lampposts adorning every landing.

Accessing the Church

There is no cost to visit Sacré Coeur, but you can expect to be funneled through a narrow gateway for the purposes of a security check. Be prepared to open your bags and jackets.

Once inside, you'll note signs indicating that seating is intended for those coming to the church to pray. If that's not your principal reason for visiting, your option is to walk around the outer aisle, into the ambulatory (behind the choir & altar areas) and eventually make your way back out.

Visiting the Dome

If you didn't get enough climbing on your way up to Sacré Coeur, and would like to do a bit more, some incredible panoramas await you at the top of the basilica.

For only 6€, it's possible to access the rooftop dome, but note that it'll take some 300 steps to get there. The stairway is, for the most part, circular and the closer you get to the top, the more confined the space. It's definitely doable, but if you suffer from claustrophobia at all, this particular part of the visit might not be the best suited for you.

The Artists' Quarter

Since you've already made the effort to get out of the city center, you may as well take a short walk over to Place du Tertre (Tertre Square).

Montmartre is a well-known artists' quarter and between Sacré Coeur and the square you'll have yet more choice of souvenir shops and restaurants (you can even find some take-out up there if you're eating on the run).

Place du Tertre boasts a number of great restaurants as well as a small army of artists willing to sketch your portrait in various media, from simple charcoal portraits to color portraits and even paper cut-outs of your profile.

From here you're also only steps away from a Starbucks location as well, but more on that in the next chapter.

Leaving Montmartre

If you're already at Place du Tertre, rather than heading back to the basilica to get back down, you have the option of descending the stairway on rue du Calvaire, turning left on rue Gabrielle and making your way back to the base of the rue Foyatier stairway and Montmartre Funicular, and therefore, to the top of rue Steinkerque, allowing you a quick return to the Anvers metro station.

The Louvre

Metro: Palais Royale – Musée du Louvre

Ahh... the Louvre. Some of you will want to see it because there's an inner art buff that is just dying to drink in the flawless marble statues or the paintings by various masters. Others will want to see it simply because that's something that one doesn't go to Paris and *not* do. Either way, that's fine, it's an incredible building that indisputably houses one of the world's greatest collections.

Let me begin by making a couple of disclaimers

1. It *is* possible to do a quick visit of the Louvre. In 2015, I took a group of 45 young people to the city and their to-do list was long for a one day visit, but the Louvre was a non-negotiable. 2 ½ hours was allocated to the Louvre for those who really wanted to do it. It was a bit of a race and they of course did not get to fully appreciate everything, but they did get to see the Mona Lisa and other great works.
2. If you're a die-hard art fan and want to not only get the biggest bang for your buck but to also be able to fully appreciate what you're seeing, you really want to dedicate the better part of a day to the Louvre.
3. Get there early. The line-ups can quickly grow to an impressive length as can the ensuing wait time.
4. If your main goal in going to the Louvre is to see the Mona Lisa (or "la Jaconde" as she's called in French), be forewarned, she's not the giant canvas that many expect to find. Rather, she is quite small in proportion; only 77 x 53cm (30" x 21"). She is encased in glass and depending on crowd size, it can be tough to get up close for a good look.

Now, let me give you some information.

Hours of Operation

The Louvre is open every day from 9am until 6pm (until 10pm on Wednesdays and Fridays). Various galleries will begin to close thirty minutes prior to those times. The museum is closed on Tuesdays.

The principal entrances are through the Pyramid (located in the middle open courtyard) and via the Carousel du Louvre (an underground shopping hall beneath the courtyard).

The only two holidays that the Louvre is closed, aside from the regular Tuesday closures, is May 1 (Labor Day in France) and December 25.

Cost of Entry:

Tickets to the Louvre are 15€. Children under the age of 18 are able to visit with no charge and European residents, between the ages of 18 and 25 can also visit for free (upon presentation of official ID).

Also note that the first Sunday of every month, between October and March (incl.) there is no entrance fee. You can visit for free.

For more information:
www.louvre.fr/en

PARIS 3 DAYS NO STRESS: A Travel Guide

Notre Dame Cathedral

Metro: Île de la Cité **or** Saint-Michel – Notre Dame

You'll note that I've suggested two different metro stops to access Notre Dame.

I've included Saint Michel–Notre Dame because it bears the name of the famous cathedral and has the advantage that, upon exiting the metro station, you're almost immediately upon the Seine, in view of the church.

Typically, however, I access Notre Dame via the Île de la Cité metro station. Not only does it put you directly on the island between Notre Dame and the Sainte Chapelle, but it also puts you above ground right at the Paris flower market, Place Louis Lépine, in operation since 1830. On Sundays you'll find many of the stalls transformed into an extensive bird market.

Access

There is no charge to visit Notre Dame, however be prepared to wait in line to visit the famed cathedral. The line-up winds itself through the open square but generally moves quite quickly.

Caution: beware of individuals approaching you to

complete a survey or give to a cause. Often they are, or are working with, pickpockets. Simply don't acknowledge them or brush them aside with a casual "Non, merci" then look away.

When you arrive at the gate and the door of the cathedral, expect a security check and be prepared to open bags, purses and jackets.

Similar to Sacré Coeur, most visitors will circle around the outer aisles of the church, taking in the intricate work and stained glass in the side chapels and making their way through the ambulatory. You won't want to, nor will you be able to, miss the great rose windows in the north and south transepts.

Seating is more accessible in Notre Dame than in Sacré Coeur, although guests are reminded that it is first and foremost a place of prayer, so a measured of respect and quiet demeanor are both expected and greatly appreciated, both by staff as well as other guests.

Note, too, that flash photography is discouraged inside Notre Dame, as is generally the case in all indoor monuments and museums.

Finally, it's worth nothing that all roadway distances in France are measured *from* Notre Dame cathedral, making it kilometer zero for all highways and byways throughout the country, leading to and from the capital.

Extras

Besides the visit of the church itself, there are a few extras that make great additions to your time at Notre Dame.

1. **Pigeon Feeding:** Want to feed the pigeons and get a great photo doing so? You will often find people ready to put a bit of birdseed into your

hands in exchange for 1€. They will call the birds over, attracting them to you and you may soon find yourself with birds on your hands, arms, shoulders and head. Just remember, one of the hazards of pigeons in proximity is pigeon droppings. It's a risk, but hey...they're Parisian pigeons so you can be sure they'll do it with class!

2. **The Bell Tower:** It's possible to visit Notre Dame's bell tower but the entrance is located outside and to the left of the cathedral on rue du Cloître Notre Dame. There are over 380 steps to climb and the cost is 10€. I'd recommend asking whether or not it's free for those under 26 years old. Sometimes the courtesy is limited to Europeans only and sometimes for any visitor.

Garnier Opera

Metro: Opera

Being who I am, I can't *not* include the Garnier Opera in this book. It is my all-time favorite place to spend a few hours.

If you're thinking "I'm not into opera," no worries, you don't have to be into opera to appreciate this incredible building. In fact, operas aren't even staged there anymore, rather they are typically staged at the Opéra Bastille, the

Garnier being primarily reserved for ballet productions.

The value in visiting this monument is in seeing an incredible example of pure opulence in architecture and design.

Design Details

The architect, Charles Garnier, was an artist in the truest sense of the term. As an example, the width of the great foyer was calculated, not according to building proportionality norms at the time, but rather according to the average width of a lady's formal attire. Not taken by itself, it was assumed that a true lady would be accompanied by at least two other people at any given time. If this was to be a place of relaxed strolling, then the architect would need to make allowance, in the width of the room, for at least three groups of three people to meet and pass one another without any impediment to fluid movement. Such was the thought process of this architectural artist.

What's more, if you note the number of balconies in the grand staircase, you must know the reason behind them. Garnier maintained that, in an opera, the spectacle did not begin on the stage, but the moment that the first patrons walked through the door. Hence, the balconies were placed to allow not only for semi-private conversation but also to allow the curious to watch that spectacle played out by fellow opera goers as they ascended and descended the stairway with great pomp and circumstance.

As you can see, the art of people watching goes back a long way. If you are a people watcher yourself, then you are in good company!

Visiting

Typically, when I visit, I like to simply pay the 11€ entry

fee for an unguided visit and make my way around. I've visited enough times already and have read a couple of books on the theatre, so I often just go in with my journal or postcards to write, or even a book to read for a while. I just like being immersed in that atmosphere.

On an unaccompanied visit, you will also be able to see all the main areas and take some spectacular photos (avoid flash photography). On rare occasions, the theatre hall itself will be closed, particularly if they are setting up for a performance. There have been a few times I've been there when the balcony on the front façade, the loggia, has been closed as well.

Must-Sees

If time is limited, be sure to see the following areas:

1. Members' Rotunda: You will automatically come through this area after purchasing your ticket. I suggest you go to the center of the room and look up at the filigree work in the central ceiling medallion. You will see, very intricately incorporated, the full name of the architect, "Jean Louis Charles Garnier" and the dates of the opera's construction "1861 – 1875."

2. Grand Staircase: This is a great spot for taking pictures… either on the staircase itself or on one of the numerous marble balconies overlooking the staircase.

3. Grand Foyer: This is the room described above in. It is an absolutely stunning room and can be a little tricky for taking pictures in because of the lighting, but with a bit of patience, you'll get some good ones. Don't forget to look up at the incredible ceiling. On either end of the foyer you'll find the Sun and Moon Rotundas.

4. Library: This is tucked away down the hallway on the rue Auber side of the building and can be accessed through the Moon Rotunda, itself accessible from either the Grand Foyer or the hallway surrounding the Grand Staircase. You'll see the permanent collection of music scores as well as models of various stage settings.

5. Loggia: This is the arched balcony on the front façade of the building, facing Place de l'Opéra. It is not always open, but when it is it offers a superb view of the Avenue de l'Opéra and the Café de la Paix. If by chance there are buskers playing on the steps of the opera, you'll have the best seats in the house. If busker Youri Menna is playing… you'll hear one of the most beautiful busker voices in Paris and you'll get your money's worth out of one of his 10€ CDs.

6. Auditorium: Unless you've purchased a guided tour, your only access to the auditorium will be through two boxes on the mane level (same level as the Grand Foyer). You get to feel what it would've been like to watch a ballet presentation from the rich red-velveted, and quite private, boxes. With their recessed cloakroom area, it is easy to see how a night out at the theatre provided quite a setting for private discussions… or were they rendezvous?

7. Box 5 (la loge 5): Box 5 was supposed to have been reserved for the exclusive use of the Phantom of the Opera in Gaston LeRoux's classic-gone-broadway.

Bargain-Priced Performance Tickets

If you happen to be in town on a day where there is a production at the Garnier Opera, it may be possible to get last minute seats for as low as 10€. These tickets, if available, are only sold on the day of the performance and will have quite a limited view.

For more information on bargain tickets:
www.operadeparis.fr/en

PARIS 3 DAYS NO STRESS: A Travel Guide

search for the **FAQs**

For more information on visiting the Garnier Opera
www.operadeparis.fr/en/visits/palais-garnier

Love Locks

Metro: Pont Neuf

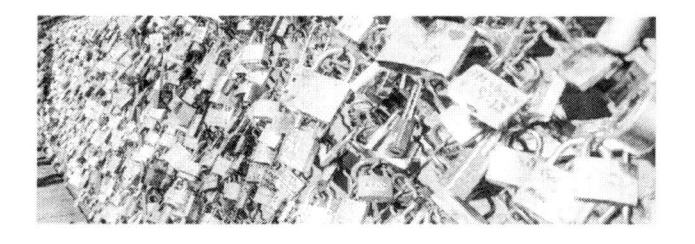

You've heard of them and perhaps you've determined to place a love lock of your own on Paris' famous Pont des Arts, dubbed the Pont des Amoureux (the Lovers' Bridge).

The love lock phenomenon was so popular among tourists *(Parisians dislike them)*, it proved to be a public safety hazard. The railing panels of the bridge became so heavy under the weight of thousands of locks, that several panels simply fell off, tumbling into the Seine River below, like the keys to many a heart… also part of the tradition.

Those panels began being dismantled in 2015 and have since been replaced by transparent and translucent panels upon which it's impossible to attach new locks.

With the inability to place them on the Pont des Arts, they've begun to spring up elsewhere, but the practice is strongly discouraged as it degrades public property.

> **Get-the-feeling tip:**
>
> While you may have trouble attaching a love lock to the Pont des Arts, you may have less trouble finding an accordion player ready to serenade you as you enjoy the view of boats passing beneath. For a few Euro's tip (the price of a love-lock), he may even agree to let you take a selfie with him. Accordion music goes hand in hand with Paris. If you're prepared to pay him a little something ask him to play "Sous les ponts de Paris" ('Neath the bridges of Paris).

Bouqinistes

Metro: Pont Neuf, Pont Marie **or** Saint-Michel Notre Dame

Traditionally, the bouquinistes are booksellers (the French word "bouquin" is a familiar word for "book") who display their wares in little green boxes attached to the walls along the quais, and typically open up during the late mornings and afternoons.

Though there are some nine hundred boxes in Paris, you won't find them just anywhere. They are primarily located in the vicinity of Île de la Cité, although you won't find them on the island itself; they are on the left and right banks of the Seine.

Initially the bouquinistes were peddlers of used or antique books. In more recent years however, they have diversified and some offer up a selection of magazines, prints of Paris paintings, souvenirs, postcards and other memorabilia.

Arc de Triomphe

Metro: Charles-de-Gaulle Étoile

The Arc de Triomphe is, without question one of the iconic landmark monuments of Paris and is prominently placed atop the elevated west end of the Champs Élysées. In a straight line out from the Louvre and the Tuilleries Gardens, the arch was the brainchild of French Emperor Napoleon, in 1806. At the base of the arch lies the tomb of the unknown soldier, the flam of which is rekindled every evening at 6:30pm.

Impressive from every angle around the giant Place Charles-de-Gaulle, visitor must go beneath the *Place* in order to access the monument.

Details

Tickets are 12€ but entry is free for children under the age of 18 and even for European residents between the ages of

18 and 25 (all upon presentation of official ID of course).

You purchase tickets beneath the arch, re-ascend to street level and present your tickets when accessing either the stairs of the elevator (see below).

The monument is open 'generally' 360 days per year but you can consult their website for specific dates of planned closures. Exceptional closures can also be caused by weather periodically.

Access

Note that there are two accessible levels to the arch.

The museum portion is an indoor visitors area accessible by a circular stairway of 284 steps. This area is also accessible via an elevator for those with reduced mobility.

From the museum area you can also visit the observation deck, on top of the monument, via another 46 steps. From here you can expect to see the million-dollar, 360 degree, panoramic view of Paris... looking right down the Champs Élysées to the Louvre or, off to your right, toward the Eiffel Tower and the Tour Montparnasse beyond.

For more information:
www.paris-arc-de-triomphe.fr/en

Outside of Town

If you have extra time and would like to get out of Paris, there are other possibilities such as.

- **Disneyland Paris**
  Main Street USA in the heart of France
- **Palace of Versailles**
  Louis XIV's hunting lodge

PARIS 3 DAYS NO STRESS: A Travel Guide

- **Palace of Fontainebleau**
  Most closely associated with Napoleon Bonaparte

Companies like **Paris City Vision** also offer day trips to the Loire Valley and castles like the Château de Chambord whose gardens were completely redone in 2016-2017.

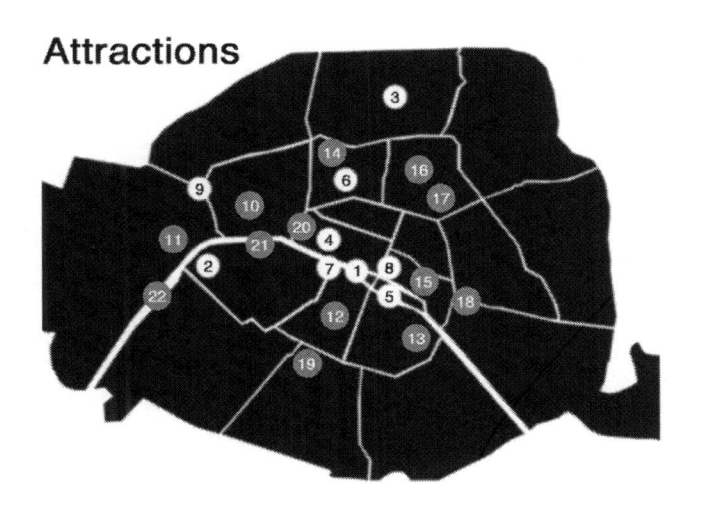

Attractions

○ Primary Attraction
(described in detail)

● Secondary Attraction
(Mentioned in text)

1. Sightseeing Tours
   Vedettes du Pont Neuf
2. Eiffel Tower
3. Sacré Coeur / Montmartre
4. The Louvre & Tuilleries
   Carousel du Louvre
5. Notre Dame
6. Garnier Opera
7. Love Locks
8. Bouquinistes
9. Arc de Triomphe
10. Champs Élysées
11. Trocadero Esplanade
12. Jardins du Luxembourg
13. Jardins des Plantes
    Quai-side dancing
14. Galleries Lafayette
15. Hôtel de Ville
16. Gare du Nord
17. Gare de l'Est
18. Gare de Lyon
19. Gare de Montparnasse
20. Place de la Concorde
21. Alexandre III Bridge
22. Statue of Liberty

MIKE LONG

7

STARBUCKS

Travelling to Paris from North America and wondering whether you'll be able to make it for a few days without grabbing a Starbucks? No fear, we've got you covered. At the time of writing, there are over forty Starbucks' locations in Paris.

I won't highlight all of them (The Starbucks' app will do that for you), but I will give you the low-down on a number of the high traffic locations, conveniently located near the major sights and monuments mentioned in the preceding chapter.

Starbucks Rewards

Are you a Starbucks Gold Member back home? Or perhaps in the process of working your war toward Gold

Status? Know that the perks and points associated with your status back home do not transfer to Starbucks France. The two are completely different companies.

Similarly, if you are Starbucks staff and accustomed to receiving bonus perks or discounts, you will not be entitled to them when visiting a French location. Again, while you can still get many of the same delicious drinks, made with just as much TLC, the companies are separate enough that privileges do not cross the Atlantic.

Starbucks Gifts

Want to bring a Starbucks souvenir back for yourself or as a gift for a friend? Just like at home, you'll have your pick of tumblers, mugs & travel mugs, but in my mind, the two best buys are:

> **Starbucks' Paris City Mug:** If you're a collector, you know what I'm talking about. You can find them with a few French city names on them (Paris, Bordeaux & Lyon) or simply with France as well.
>
> **Starbucks' Demi-Tasse Gift Set:** This set of two demi-tasses are similar in design to the full-sized city mugs, except smaller… think espresso size! One says Paris and features the Eiffel Tower, while the second says France and features the Mont St. Michel. The set makes a great gift because from a price point perspective, it is less than 10€ and because of its small size, it'll save room in your suitcase or carry-on.

Location, Location, Location!

As a reminder, the list below is not intended to be exhaustive, but to give you an idea of where you can find a Starbucks location in proximity to some of the *must-see* monuments around the city. Ready? Let's go!

Louvre

Metro: Palais Royal – Musée du Louvre

The most conveniently placed Starbucks, in relation to the Louvre, is inside the Carousel du Louvre, an underground shopping mall accessible from rue de Rivoli.

Be prepared to pass through a security check upon entering. You'll go down two sets of stairs / escalators and be walking toward a giant inverted pyramid which double as a skylight and great photo spot. Starbucks is roughly halfway down the corridor on the left.

This is a very busy location so seating will often be at a premium if you happen to be there during peak seasons. You can often find a spot (depending on how many people are in your group) but you may have to wait a little bit.

The second location in proximity to the Louvre, is the Échelle location, located on the corner of rue de Rivoli and rue de l'Échelle.

You'll find it easily enough as it's located right across the street from a small McDonalds location (184 rue de Rivoli) and while it's not located in the Louvre, it is still a busy location given its proximity to the famous palace and the many souvenir shops situated along rue de Rivoli. There is, however, also more seating in this location.

L'Opéra Garnier

Metro: Opera

The most famous Café parisien near the Garnier Opera is the Café de la Paix, a pricey but legendary French bistro. If you're ready to forego the French icon in favor of the Seattle-based icon, then your closest location is **Capucines** (3 boulevard des Capucines).

When you exit the Opera metro station, with the Garnier Opera to your back, you'll go left a short way down boulevard des Capucines where you'll find Starbucks on your right.

Galleries Lafayette / Printemps

Metro: Chausée d'Antin LaFayette

If you're planning to visit one of the most historic department stores in Paris (which I highly recommend) then you can rest your weary feet on the 3rd floor of the main building (Lafayette Dome) while overlooking one of the glitziest perfume aisles in the city. Above you, the incredible stained glass dome, itself reason enough to visit this department store.

This location has the least available seating of any Starbucks locations that I've seen in Paris. If you're visiting with a friend, you'll definitely want to have them scout for seats while you're placing the drink order.

If you're scared you come across like a vulture hovering, don't be. Someone else is likely also hovering (perhaps a bit further away) and indeed, the person preparing to vacate the chair likely hovered in order to get it in the first place.

Just smile and say "Sorry, I don't mean to hover, but… you know, seats are few and far between!" or, in French, "Désolé, mais vous comprenez… il y a si peu de places."

Montmartre / Sacré Coeur

Metro: Abesses **or** Anvers

Note: for the purpose of consistency, I indicate two "nearby" metro stations, but given the location of Sacré Coeur and Starbucks, high on Montmartre, these metro stations are for reference only, you can expect a good fifteen minute walk or more, uphill.

Starbucks can be found at 8-10 rue Norvins but it might be easier to use Place du Tertre as your reference point.

Place du Tertre is extremely well known, not only for the number of restaurants that can be found there, but also for the number of artists who are only too willing to sketch your portrait for a price.

There is a generous amount of seating at this location and it's generally not difficult to find a spot.

Arc de Triomphe

Metro: Charles de Gaulle - Étoile

This Starbucks is located at 23 avenue de Wagram. It's a smaller location with seating both inside and on the sidewalk, but your personal space will be limited – particularly inside. That being said, some of the most personable and jovial staff I've encountered are at this location (perhaps owing to the fact that I was there during the Christmas season).

If you've walked up the Champs Élysées, and are facing the Arc de Triomphe, Wagram will be the third avenue on your right; it's perpendicular to les Champs Élysées.

There are twelve streets that converge at the Arc de Triomphe so you may have to look a bit, but by way of offering a helping hand, between Champs Élysées and Wagram there are two streets coming off the intersection like spokes on a bicycle wheel (these two are avenue de Friedland and avenue Hoche).

Eiffel Tower

Metro: La Tour-Maubourg

Note: "La Tour Maubourg" is NOT the nearest metro station to the Eiffel Tower (see previous chapter) but the nearest to the Starbucks location referenced below.

Unlike many of the other touristy hot-spots in Paris, and unfortunately, there isn't a terribly convenient Starbucks location near to the Eiffel Tower.

The closest is at 90 rue St. Dominique, but expect a good 15-minute walk to get there as it's located roughly half way between the Eiffel Tower (Champs de Mars) and the Hôtel des Invalides (Where Napoleon is buried).

Train Stations

If, by chance, you're planning to take a train out of the city for any reason, you'll be able to grab a Starbucks to go at the following major rail stations:

- **Gare du Nord** (18 rue de Dunkerque)
- **Gare de l'Est** (rail level, Pl. 11 Novembre 1918)
- **Gare de Lyon** (plateforme Bleu : Pl. L. Armand)
- **Gare Montparnasse** (17 boulevard de Vaugirard)
- **Gare St. Lazare** (14 rue Interieure)

Need More?

As I mentioned at the beginning of this chapter, this list is not intended to be exhaustive but simply an overview of locations near the major sights. If you'd like to search out even more locations, let me suggest two options:

1. Visit www.Starbucks.fr's store locator for Paris
2. Use the **Starbucks app** on your smartphone

    (use the app on your smartphone only if you have a data plan that will not incur excessive roaming charges and be sure to enable location services)

Name Please?

Ever had your name misspelled by an otherwise brilliant Starbucks barista? Well, there are some things that don't change from one side of the Atlantic to the other. Some non-French names will present a challenge for even the most seasoned French barista.

If there's a possibility that your name might be misspelled anyway, why not just flow with it from the outset and give yourself a French name? Not only does it minimize the chance of your name being misspelled, it allows you to take on an entirely new identity while in the French capital

Here are some suggestions along with their pronunciation:

Ladies:

- Brigitte — Bree-shjeet
- Élise — Ay-leez
- Stéphanie — Stay-fa-nee
- Mathilde — Mah-tild
- Chloé — Kloh-ay

Gentlemen:

- Louis — Loo-ee
- Théo — Tay-oh
- Maël — My-el
- Kylian — Kee-lee-un
- Dylan — Dee-lunn

Note: IF you choose to go with a French name... just don't forget to pick up your drink when they call you by your new name!

There you have it. You're now assured to have a good caffeine rush coursing through your veins, giving you the energy needed to see all there is to see during your visit.

One Final Note on Coffee

Although Starbucks is a familiar taste of home and it's great to be able to grab one, don't let this be your only coffee stop during your time in Paris.

One of the most Parisian things imaginable is to sit at one of the sidewalk cafés and order one of the following:

- Un p'tit café	Espresso
- Une noisette	Espresso w/hint of milk
- Un café au lait	Coffee w/milk
- Un cappuccino	Same as at home!

Don't be so determined to get a good 20oz Starbucks that you pass up experiencing "un p'tit café parisien".

Finally, though hours of operation can vary slightly between locations (check your app or the website mentioned above for specifics) it's safe to say that most locations close much earlier than would be the case in North America. It's not uncommon for a Starbucks location to close even at 8:00pm.

The reason? Likely because between 7-8pm is a fairly standard supper time for most French and given that meals typically last longer than what might be common elsewhere, there is little chance that people will be coming in for a cuppa joe after supper.

Here's a map of the Starbucks locations mentioned.

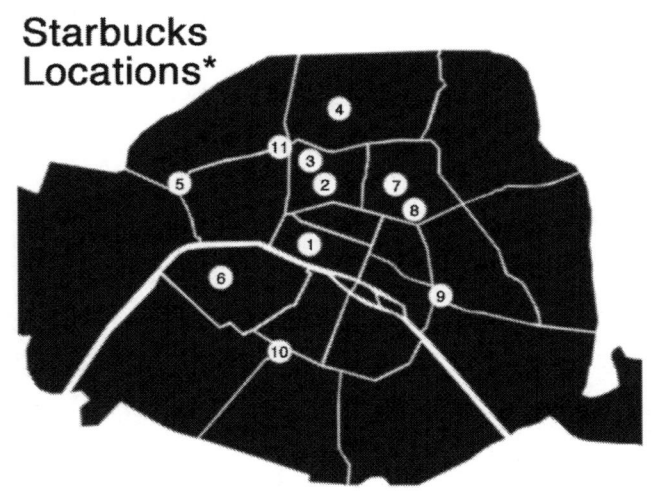

Starbucks Locations*

1. Carrousel du Louvre
2. Opéra Garnier
3. Galleries Lafayette (Dôme)
4. Montmartre - Sacré Coeur
5. Arc de Triomphe (Wagram)
6. La Tour-Mauberg
7. Gare du Nord
8. Gare de l'Est
9. Gare de Lyon
10. Gare de Montparnasse
11. Gare Saint-Lazare

(Again, Note that this is far from an exhaustive list. It shows only the Starbucks' locations in proximity to the Attractions mentioned in Chapter 6 and some of the major train stations.)

8

UNIQUE ADD-ONS

In this chapter I want to include a few things that don't necessarily constitute attractions or monuments but which could add a certain special touch to your time in Paris.

I've categorized them according to three budget levels:

1. Frugal
2. Level-headed
3. Extravagant

I find the majority of sights and attractions to be reasonably priced in the Paris area so the Level Headed section will have fewer things than the Frugal and the Extravagant sections.

Here's to adding a few extras to your time in Paris!

FRUGAL

If you wish to stretch your travel dollar to the max, then know that you need not forego everything once you arrive… opting to only stroll outdoors and take pictures of the parks and building exteriors.

Free Fashion Shows
(Galleries Lafayette)

Metro: Chaussée d'Antin - Lafayette

Every Friday the Galleries Lafayette flagship store (Lafayette Coupole) offers the possibility of attending a 30min fashion show on the fourth floor, at no cost (unless you're part of a group of 15 or more). The one condition is that you **must** reserve your spot ahead of time by emailing:

FashionShow@GalleriesLafayette.com

Shows take place at 3pm and although it's small enough that most all seats are good, I advise arriving between 2:30 and 2:45 for the best seating.

For more information:
Haussmann.galerieslafayette.com/en/fashionshow

Free Museum Entry

On the first Sunday of each month, many museums and attractions do not charge an entry fee.

My main goal here is to simply make you aware of the tip. For a very good list of which museums offer this advantage, I'm going to refer you to the official website of

PARIS 3 DAYS NO STRESS: A Travel Guide

the Paris Visitor and Convention Bureau:

en.parisinfo.com and search for "Paris for Free"

On that site, they'll refer you to museums which are free:

- Every day, all year 'round.
- The first Sunday of the month (year 'round)
- The first Sunday of the month (at specific periods)

The Louvre, for example, only offers free entry the first Sunday of the month between October 1 and March 31.

Note: If you're under 26 and a resident of the European Union, many museums, châteaux and exhibits are always free for you including the Louvre and Versailles for example.

Paris for Free

Let me come back to Paris' Visitor & Convention Bureau website for a moment. Besides indicated free entry to various museums, there's an entire section entitled **Paris for Free** where you can get tips on:

- Free events and cultural outings
- A free meal at a bar or restaurant
- Free things to do with kids
- Under their **10 Free things to do in Paris** section, they'll even tell you how you can get a free haircut or makeover. But, they caution, be prepared to come out with a whole new look!

For more information:
en.parisinfo.com

Search "Paris for Free" and
"10 Free things to do in Paris"

Bargain priced Opera Tickets

As I mentioned in the previous chapter, it's sometimes possible to get same-day, last-minute tickets at the Garnier Opera for as low as 10€. It will depend on availability of course and your view of the stage will be quite restricted. Nonetheless, it would be an experience to talk about.

LEVEL HEADED

The main thing I want to share with you in this section is the smartphone app The Fork (also at www.theFork.com). It's not going to give you freebies but it can save you're a few extra Euros on some restaurant bills.

TheFork.com

If you've never used this website/app, it's a reservation service for restaurants in countries around the world. By reserving through the site (you must be a registered user) you can get your meals at a discounted price.

For Paris, you simply indicate where in Paris you'd like to eat (by exact address of by arrondissement), what kind of cuisine you prefer and roughly what time you'd like to eat. It will then propose a list of participating restaurants in the area and the deals that they offer.

One thing to note is this, given the French custom of eating late (7-8pm), you will find great deals if you reserve a bit earlier. Since it's not uncommon for North Americans to eat closer to 5-6pm it works out well. I've gotten up to 50% off my main courses by eating in that early window. Note that discounts aren't necessarily applied to the entire bill. Some restaurants may offer a percentage off the meal itself (drinks & desserts excluded), others may offer a free dessert, etc. The key is to familiarize yourself with the terms and conditions of the deal offered by your chosen restaurant ahead of time.

Why include this in the Level Headed section as opposed to the Frugal section if it involves a discount? Simply put, since TheFork.com generally proposes restaurant dining, you can still expect to pay a decent price on your overall bill (Note: the typical price per person is usually listed on the restaurant description).

Sightseeing Cruises:
(Vedettes du Pont Neuf)

I mentioned in chapter 6, but just in case you missed it, you can get between 2€ and 4€ off a 14€ ticket price when you book your tickets online and in advance. You can find full details on their website:

www.vedettesdupontneuf.com

EXTRAVAGANT

If this is a once-in-a-lifetime visit and you'd like to add one or more very special experiences, then below you'll find a few ideas that will do just that!

Paris Authentic

This company offers tours of Paris in France's legendary Deux Cheveaux car (2CV – or two horse-power), one of the first mass produced and highly popular cars to take the country by storm.

Daytime tours range from one to six and ½ hours and can be combined with a boat tour, while the evening tours are generally shorter but can also be extended by combining with a dinner cruise for example.

Their site, ParisAuthentic.om presents the prices based on a 2 passenger fare, but it is possible to have three passengers as well. When you click on the excursion of your choice, it offers up a per-person rate (the overall per-person rate is lower in the case of 3 passengers, but not the overall trip rate).

As an example, at the time of printing:

2hr daytime Classic Tour = 179€
89€/person (2 passeng.) or 63€/person (3 passeng.)

2hr nighttime Montmartre Tour = 189€
94€/person (2 passeng.) or 66€/person (3 passeng.)

Note: pricing is illustrative only and is by no means binding on Paris Authentic, should their pricing change.

Paris Picnic

Want a memorable lunchtime picnic without the fuss of have to grocery shop, prepare and pack yourself? **ParisPicnic.com** has the answer!

Open every day from noon until 3:30pm (except Wednesday and Thursday), they'll set you up with everything you'll need including utensils and a cotton blanket to sit on; yours to keep. They'll even deliver it to various parks in the city center.

Prices start at 32€ per person for Le Classique and 57.50€ per person for Le Chic (including champagne, foie gras and macarons). Beyond that, they'll even prepare a surprise setup and photo session, for a premium. Something extra special for an extra special occasion.

Dinner Cruises

There are a number of companies that offer a dining experience on the Seine River. I'm going to highlight the company **Bateaux Parisiens** because my wife and I enjoyed a romantic evening dinner cruise with them several years ago on an escape weekend from the kids.

At lunchtime you can expect a relaxed 2hr dinner cruise to cost from 59€ - 89€ per person, depending on where you'd like to be seated and your desired level of service.

They also have several evening dinner cruises, some longer than others. I recommend the 2h30min cruise (the one that we did). Prices for this cruise range from 99€ for the basic level of service with non-window seating, all the way up to 205€ per person for their premium menu and level of service.

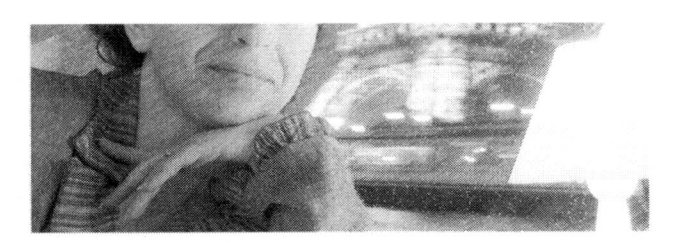

Their website gives very clear visuals as to seating and explanations of their levels of service.

We had an absolutely wonderful dinner cruise with them and would recommend it without hesitation!

For more information see
www.bateauxparisiens.com/en

9

MISC. TIPS

What follows are some general tips to consider. A few of them will be relevant for travel in general and others are specific to visiting Paris.

GOING GREEN

Want to eat organic? You'll find 100% organic produce at two local weekend markets: the Marché des Batignolles (8th arrondissement, Metro: Place de Clichy, open Saturdays 9am-3pm) and the Marché Biologique de Raspail (6th arrondissement, Metro: Notre Dame des Champs, open Sundays 9am-3pm).

Want to discover other Eco-Friendly aspects of Paris? There are a number of activities listed on the following official website:

en.parisinfo.com search for "Green Paris"

Activities include walking tours, a schedule of eco-friendly activities and festivals as well as unusual parks and gardens.

Les Champs Élysées are car-free on the first Sunday of each month according to Paris' Visitor & Convention Bureau.

Paris Plages: For a few weeks each summer, some of the *quais* are transformed into sandy beaches, complete with beach umbrellas, live music and children's play areas. Look for it between late July and mid August.

LANGUAGE

Don't know how to speak French? No worries! Most service providers are familiar enough with catering to international travelers that they have at least enough English to complete a sales transaction. I would, however, recommend always beginning your interaction with *"Bonjour Madame"* or *"Bonjour Monsieur"*, even if you continue in English afterward.

Greeting them in their language shows courtesy and respect for who *they* are and where *you* are. You'd be surprised how a little can sometimes go a long way.

ABRUPT VENDORS / STAFF

Astute souvenir vendors will roll out the red carpet to you as a tourist, but not all are astute. There are several areas where souvenir shops line one or both sides of the street for several blocks. Vendors know that if you don't buy from them, someone else will come right after you. For this reason, you may not always find them to be as warm and welcoming as they may be elsewhere. In addition, "The customer is always right." mentality doesn't always apply in Paris. If you experience it, don't take it personally.

SECURITY

Travel Documents

It's always a good idea to have a photocopy of your travel documents when you travel and keep them separate from your actual documents. Better yet, before leaving, scan important documents (passport, airline tickets, credit card information, travel insurance, etc.) and store the scanned copies in Dropbox, Google Drive (or another online storage program) or even in your email.

While we're on the subject of travel precautions, take photos of your luggage before starting your trip. Should it get lost *en route*, having pictures makes it easier to open a lost-luggage claim.

VigiPirate

This is the name for France's national security alert system. You will see the red, white and black, triangular logo at many of the main monuments and administrative buildings. Although in place for several years, it has become much more visible in Paris since the two major attacks of 2015. The plan is always in place so don't be surprised if you are asked to:

- present your bags for inspection
- open your jacket or bulky clothing
- pass through a metal detector

Knowing these things in advance can help you plan for your day, keep it in mind when choosing what to wear.

Pickpockets

Personally, I have never been the victim of pickpockets or any other similar problem in Paris, but I've seen pickpockets at work and have seen security forces intervene to assist unsuspecting tourists.

If you see small groups of young women (2-4) with either clipboards or sheets of paper approaching people in an effort to engage them in conversation, **avoid them**. Do not even make eye contact. Sometimes it's a survey and other times it's a request for money for some good cause, but in all cases, it's a distraction and the opportunity for you to find yourself in trouble.

I've most frequently seen them in and around the Eiffel Tower / Trocadero area, Notre Dame, the Louvre and rue de Rivoli, but that doesn't mean that you won't see them elsewhere.

Metro

When in the metro, and depending on the time of day, you can easily find yourself in cramped quarters. Here are five things to always keep in mind:

1. Where is your wallet or purse located?
2. Is your purse, knapsack or bag zipped or unzipped, open or closed?
3. If your coat pockets don't zipper shut, place valuables (keys, wallets, etc.) in an **inside** pocket.
4. Gentlemen, **IF** you keep your wallet in your pants' pocket (which I do not recommend), keep it in a front pocket.
5. If possible, have bags, purses or knapsacks in front of you or, if seated, on your lap.

"An ounce of prevention is worth a pound of cure"

If you find yourself standing in line somewhere waiting to get into a monument or taking photos, some of the same tips are equally useful. It's often just a question of being very aware of your surroundings.

Separated in the Metro?

If you are traveling in a group, you need to plan for the eventuality of being separated in the metro.

Our policy has always been this: IF, while getting on a metro train, part of the group is able to get on the train and the other part of the group is not. (It's crowded, you can't all get on and the doors suddenly close, for example).

- Whoever *did* get on the train simply gets off at the very next stop and wait on the platform.
- Those who were unable to get on **know** that they are not *"lost"* but that the rest of their party will be waiting for them at the next stop.
- This reduces fear and panic for everyone.

BANKS CARDS & RFID

One of the things that can add an extra level of protection to your touring about Paris is the purchase of RFID sleeves for your bank cards.

If you've ever been able to pay for an item simply by using tap-to-pay (ie. Without inserting your cards and entering your PIN), then your bank card is RFID enabled, meaning that key identity and banking information is visible to RFID readers or those who possess them and come in very close proximity to you (think: Crowds).

The hazard is that someone could appear to bump into you, but their real motive is to get close enough for an RFID reader to potentially pick up your bank card information.

How to protect yourself?

First of all, know that rarely is anything 100% avoidable, but there are precautions you can take to minimize the risk. Here are three tips, listed from least expensive and moving up.

1. **An Altoids can:** According to makeuseof.com, keeping your bank cards in a closed Altoids can, will protect them from inadvertent scanning.
2. **RFID Sleeve:** Most luggage retailers, since they're business is to equip people who travel, will carry RFID sleeves: small, inexpensive foil sleeves into which you slide your cards.
3. **RFID Wallet:** These too can be purchased from luggage retailers and vary in price from $10-$40 (or more, depending on your taste).

There are supporters for RFID protection and detractors who say that yet another industry is being built around people's fear. That being said, these solutions are fairly inexpensive and provide an extra level of protection.

IN GENERAL

Although I've mentioned a number of things that fall into the "security" bucket, please don't be overly alarmed by the cautions I've suggested. You are no more at risk from pickpockets in Paris than you would be in any major world city. Again, I've never yet fallen victim to any of these mishaps personally, but again,

> "an ounce of prevention is worth a pound of cure."

PARIS 3 DAYS NO STRESS: A Travel Guide

TOP 10 "DID YOU KNOWS"

1. **The Luxor Obelisk** (place de la Concorde)**:** is the oldest monument in Paris at 3,300 years old. It is also a giant sundial.

2. **The Louvre:** Spending one minute at each of the 35,000 works of art housed there, for eight hours per day, it would take three months to see it all.

3. **Housing:** Want to buy an apartment in downtown Paris? Think again. The average price per square meter is 9,400.00€ or roughly $1,000.00 per square foot (as of January 2017)… without counting utilities!

4. **Building Bridges:** In Paris, a total of 37 bridges cross the Seine River. The most ornate is the Pont Alexandre III (A gift from Russia, it bears the coats of arms of both St. Petersburg and Paris) while the oldest bridge is ironically named le Pont Neuf (the New Bridge).

5. **The Arc of Triumph:** is not the only one of its kind in Paris. By far the largest and most prominently placed, there are actually four arches. The three others are:

    - **Le Carrousel** – located between the Louvre and the Tuilleries Gardens.
    - **La Porte Saint-Denis** – located in the 10th arrondissement, just south of the Gare de l'Est.
    - **La Porte Saint-Martin** – located less than a kilometer away from the Porte Saint-Denis.

    These last two were gates to the old walls of the city.

6. **"Room" in the Inn:** Did you know it's possible to get a free spot to sleep for the night in Paris? It's true, but "room" is in quotation marks for a reason.

    - **The Location:** Shakespeare and Company bookstore, Rive Gauche.
    - **The Conditions:** You have to be a writer (even beginners are welcome), there must be room available, you must read for two hours each day and write a one-page autobiography for their records. **Note:** Personal space is highly limited and you could be sleeping in the Fiction section.

7. **Lady Liberty's Little Sister:** Did you know that New York City's most famous statue was a gift from France? Not only that but there is a replica of Lady Liberty located at the end of l'Île aux Cygnes (Swan Island), not far from the Eiffel Tower.

8. **Paris Underground:** Besides the Paris metro, there is another network of underground tunnels beneath southern Paris, of which the Catacombs are only one part. Years of mining white limestone left some 170 miles of tunnels beneath the southern boroughs. A literal underground culture has developed and, in 2004, according to a 2016 article in Britain's **The Telegraph**, police found a fully functioning (and totally illegal) cinema down there.

9. **A Temporary Tower:** When built for the World Fair of 1889, the Eiffel Tower was only to be a temporary structure. Now it's hard to imaging Paris without it!

10. **It's about time!** The first publicly installed clock in Paris can still be found on the wall of the Conciergerie, on Île de la Cité. A magnificent piece of craftsmanship, it began ticking in 1370.

TOP 10 HASHTAGS

If you plan on sharing your Paris photos on Instagram, then here are a few hashtags that will ensure your shots get viewed by as many eyes as possible, hopefully increasing the amount of #IGLove you get back from an admiring public.

Hashtag	Approx. # Users
#Paris	(58.1 million)
#ParisJeTaime	(1.6 million)
#ParisFashionWeek	(980,000)
#Parisian	(820,000)
#Parisienne	(670,000)
#ParisMonAmour	(440,000)
#ParisByNight	(400,000)
#ParisPhoto	(320,000)
#ParisCartePostale	(250,000)
#ParisianLife	(195,000)

In addition to the hashtags above, there are also some which, when you tag your photos with them, increase the chance that your picture will be featured on other IG accounts. These include (in no particular order).

#Hello_France	#igersParis
#TraverseFrance	#TopParisPhoto
#ParisMaVille	#IncroyableParis
#VivreParis	#ParisHelpLine
#ParisCartePostale	

Of course I'd love it if you tagged your photos with:

#Paris3DaysNoStress

10 GREAT PARIS INSTAGRAM ACCOUNTS

Want some inspiration before taking your own photos in Paris? Check out the following Instagram accounts:

@nathparis *(612K followers)*
    Self-taught photographer Nathalie Geoffroy

@parisjetaime *(246K followers)*
    Official account of the Paris Tourism Office.

@wonguy974 *(182K followers)*
    Paris photographer Olivier Wong

@paris *(150K followers)*
    Mulitple contributors; things to see & do in Paris

@igersparis *(83K followers)*
    Official IG community for the city of Paris

@paris_carte_postale *(23K followers)*
    Great Paris photos from multiple contributors

@paris_photographer *(22K followers)*
    Paris-based photographer Pierre Torset

@paris.foodguide *(18K followers)*
    The Foodguide app *(thefoodguide.de/download)* for restaurant ideas – restaurant locations indicated

@iheartparisfr *(18K followers)*
    Lifestyle & commercial photographer

@abramova_guendel *(8K followers)*
    Wedding & Lifestyle photographer.

10

TASTE OF THINGS TO COME

Thank you for making your way through to this point in what is my first published book. I hope that it helps you take advantage of a truly wonderful city that will take your breath away many times over during your stay.

In this final chapter, I want to include excerpts from the two next installments in the **Paris No Stress** series, entitled:

Paris You Take My Breath Away
&
Out of Paris: A Week on My French Farm

In **Paris You Take My Breath Away** you won't find lists of places of practical details, but rather an array of inspirational moments:

... moments when Paris took *my* breath away.
... moments when I found myself lost in wonder.
...moments I felt at home, though 5,000km away.

It is my hope that you will experience such moments during your trip because they are truly the things that stay with you after the photos have been put away. They are what I spoke of, in the introduction, when I spoke about Paris being a *feeling*. They are the things that… when other begin speaking about Paris, cause a smile to be etched on your face and a warm glow to radiate in your memory.

In **Out of Paris: A Week on My French Farm**, I'll share experiences I have in provincial France while house sitting for a French family and their thirty animals.

Let me give you a taste from each…

WAKING UP WITH PARIS
(from Paris, You Take My Breath Away)

I remember the day I rose early enough to witness Paris, that great city, waking up and rising from her slumber.

I'd taken an early commuter train from the suburbs and the wind hit my face as I exited the metro. Shopkeepers opened up, swept off their sidewalks, rolled out their racks of postcards or set up tables and chairs, preparing to serve *un p'tit café* to whoever ventured in to unfold their newspaper and reconnect to the world at large. All this, while boats glided almost silently up the Seine.

It was August, so most Parisians were out of the city on vacation and even the bouquinistes were far les numerous than usual. The streets were quiet, the intersections less chaotic and the sidewalks clearer than normal.

Despite the roomy paths on the sidewalk however, I found myself veering off, via a heavy stone stairway, and descending to walk along the *quais*. I wasn't used to not having to fend off the crowds.

It was early enough that the *quais* too, with the exception of a runner every now and again, offered me my own private space to drink in the city that has captivated writers, poets, and lovers for centuries.

Ernest Hemingway, speaking of Paris in the 1920's in *A Moveable Feast*, described a city quite different from 21st century Paris. He talks of fishermen casting their lines in the Seine from the *Square du Vert Gallant* at the western tip of *Ile de la Cité*, when the water level was just right.

As hard as it is to imagine pole-fishing in the Seine today, I can relate to the feeling that a fisherman may have experienced as they came down to the then quiet riverside. This morning, that same riverside is just as quiet and I am just as alone.

Maybe I am fishing. Maybe I too and trying to catch something just as elusive as the *goujon* (gudgeon fish) that Hemingway's cane-pole carrying fishermen sought; something to feed me, to bring sustenance and strength. Only that which I seek does not dwell in the mud, at the bottom of the river, at least I can't imagine that it does.

Do I know what I'm seeking?

This has been the longest summer of my life, fraught with many questions, much hurt and great bewilderment, but as I walk peacefully along the *quais* of the Seine, I'm in another place; if only for an hour, two… a day, and I'm thankful for the rest. This morning, Lord, you have granted me peace and I'm grateful. Oh so grateful.

Paul Tillich once said:

"Our language has wisely sensed the two sides of being alone. It has created the word loneliness to express the pain of being alone and it has created the word solitude to express the glory of being alone."

This morning, I'm experiencing solitude. I'm glorying in this time alone. I woke up to a city that is not at all frozen in time, as the postcards would lead one to believe. Paris is more than the great stone monuments and inanimate bistro tables and chairs lining the sidewalk. There is more to her than a great iron tower in the seventh arrondissement or the flying buttress supported cathedral in the fourth. Great tree-lined avenues lined with Baron Haussmanns's iconic, styled buildings are only the beginning.

Today I awoke and visited a city that is very much a living, breathing entity. In one sense we were both brought to life that morning, by the wind that greeted me with *la bise* as I exited the metro, the gulls soaring above the Seine on that same breeze, the individual residents, the few runners and the odd tourist. They all played a part in bringing that great city to life.

No, Paris is not frozen in time. It is very much alive, and to watch her come to life is a treat that everyone should experience at least once.

MIKE LONG

BREAKFAST WITH THE PEACOCK
(from Out of Paris: A Week on My French Farm)

The donkey, normally quite low-key, had apparently encountered something worthy of his exertion in the fallen limb. As I watched him across the yard, Nono came around the corner of the house and began looking in the living room window.

I say living room, but in these old French farm houses, the single large room off the hallway was really more of a combination living and dining room.

Between the large window, comprised of three French door panels of single pane glass and the low brick fireplace, there was just enough room for a short wooden cabinet upon which stood the flat-screen T.V. (which somehow seemed out of place). Directly opposite the T.V.

was a black leather love seat, wisely chosen as the leather was an ideal surface for resisting absorption of I-Koy's drool. I-Koy is the largest of two great danes.

Beyond the fireplace and against the same wall, an antique hutch and wallboard, proudly displaying mismatched dinner plates alongside a well-worn copy of LaFontaine's Fables. This was not the ornate, high-end antique hutch that one might easily think one when imagining French Provincial, it's of a much more humble profile; well suited to the farm.

Opposite the hutch, a tall *armoire* stood guard by the arched passageway leading to the kitchen, it's contents hidden from view behind the wooden panel doors. Life here was not about being on display, the armoire was simply for storage.

I sat between the armoire and the hutch, at a wooden table that had been smoothed by years of use, protected by a good coat or two of varnish and infused with years of love and fond memories.

To my left, the only other source of natural light in the room, a window which, while smaller than the tri-sectioned French door-window across the room, matched it in style. Since it was morning, the sun bathed the table in warmth and light.

I took another drink of coffee, greeted Nono through the glass and began to write. Nono the peacock, however, wasn't simply looking for a "Good morning!"

Tap, tap, tap… tap, tap… tap, tap…

"Qu'est-ce que tu veux toi, Nono? What are you looking for?"

Tap, tap, tap… tap, tap… tap, tap…

I had a sneaking suspicion I knew exactly what he wanted, but it was as though, by asking, I somehow expected him to out and out tell me.

Out to the summer kitchen I go. The second drawer

in the cabinet by the door is where, stashed unassumingly in a Tupperware container, was something of a cross between hard cat food and rabbit pellets. This was for Nono.

I grabbed a handful and went out to the stone-tiled back stoop. I say "stoop" because "terrace" seems to grand a word for this humble area, on a farm, in rural France. Yet I wonder too, if a "stoop" can be made of stone. Ignorant of and disinterested in my lexical self-interrogation, Nono saw what he was most interested in, a human coming out the back door with a closed hand held out toward him. He began to walk toward me.

Apparently I was winning him over. At first quite wary, I only saw Nono from a distance, atop the wall, perched on the roof or sleeping high in the rafters of the barn. If I happened to surprise him in the enclosure where the hens, goats and miniature pigs happily coexisted, he simply moved away, slowly but surely, never giving me the satisfaction of knowing that I'd startled him. Today however, he was walking toward me, proof that hunger is a powerful force for change.

I crouched down to assume a less threatening posture, held out my hand and slowly emptied its contents onto the stone surface. He came closer and I didn't move.

I pulled out my iPhone to sneak a picture but the shutter sound, while it didn't cause him to run away, did made him raise his head and cock it to one side.

Was the new sound a threat?

Apparently deciding that it was not, he resumed his meager feast and I pondered a move, sitting down beside him as he ate.

It was enough to make him raise and cock his head again but he didn't judge it a sufficient threat to warrant giving up on breakfast, so he allowed me to stay.

It wasn't long before I questioned my decision

though. Oh nothing to do with Nono but because the stone surface was still holding all the coolness of the morning and transferring that coolness to my posterior. Nonetheless, I wasn't moving. The coolness wasn't sufficient reason to give up on experiencing breakfast with a peacock.

ABOUT THE AUTHOR

Mike Long

…visited Paris for the first time in 1989, has lost track of the number of times he's been back and, since he's currently living in France, finds himself there regularly.

A Romantic at heart, he resonates well with the city, never tiring of exiting the Paris metro to be greeted by the breeze that seems to be ever-present. Returning to the Garnier Opera is like going back to visit an old friend.

Besides traveling, he loves gardening in France's near year-round garden-friendly climate, small backyard animals (his Dutch Bantam chickens would love a miniature goat or two… but there are limits) and mobile photography. Follow him on Instagram **@MikeLongSJ** or, for this book series **@ParisNoStress**.

Mike and his family have been living in France since 2015, working with the United Pentecostal Church International. He blogs weekly about their experience at

www.AIMLong.ca.

MIKE LONG

Also available:

Paris, You Take My Breath Away
25 Very Short (& true) Stories

published
November 2018

MIKE LONG

ONE LAST THING

If you've enjoyed this book and found it useful, I'd be grateful if you'd post a short review on Amazon. Your support makes a difference and I read all reviews in order to get your feedback and make this book better.

Thank you again for purchasing and reading…

#Paris3DaysNoStress

@ParisNoStress

www.AIMLong.ca/Paris

Made in the USA
Las Vegas, NV
08 November 2021